COMPACT *Research*

Illegal Immigration

Current Issues

Other books in the Compact Research series include:

Drugs
      Heroin
      Marijuana
      Methamphetamine
      Nicotine and Tobacco
      Performance-Enhancing Drugs

Current Issues
      Biomedical Ethics
      The Death Penalty
      Gun Control
      World Energy Crisis

Illegal Immigration

by Debra A. Miller

Current Issues

ReferencePoint
Press™

San Diego, CA

For more information, contact
ReferencePoint Press, Inc.
17150 Via del Campo Road, Suite 204
San Diego, CA 92127
www. ReferencePointPress.com

Picture Credits:
AP/Wide World Photos, 11, 18
Maury Aaseng, 32–34, 48–51, 64–68, 80–82

Series design:
Tamia Dowlatabadi

LIBRARY OF CONGRESS CATALOGING-IN-PUBLICATION DATA
Miller, Debra A. Illegal immigration / by Debra A. Miller.   p. cm. — (Compact research series) ISBN-13: 978-1-60152-009-8 (hardback) ISBN-10: 1-60152-009-3 (hardback) 1. Illegal aliens—United States—Juvenile literature. 2. United States—Emigration and immigration—Juvenile literature. I. Title. JV6483.M55 2007 304.8'73—dc22 <div align="right">2006032349</div>

Contents

❝ Where is the knowledge we have lost in information? ❞

—"The Rock," T.S. Eliot

As modern civilization continues to evolve, its ability to create, store, distribute, and access information expands exponentially. The explosion of information from all media continues to increase at a phenomenal rate. By 2020 some experts predict the worldwide information base will double every seventy-three days. While access to diverse sources of information and perspectives is paramount to any democratic society, information alone cannot help people gain knowledge and understanding. Information must be organized and presented clearly and succinctly in order to be understood. The challenge in the digital age becomes not the creation of information, but how best to sort, organize, enhance, and present information.

ReferencePoint Press developed the Compact Research series with this challenge of the information age in mind. More than any other subject area today, researching current events can yield vast, diverse, and unqualified information that can intimidate and overwhelm even the most advanced and motivated researcher. The Compact Research series offers a compact, relevant, intelligent, and conveniently organized collection of information covering a variety of current and controversial topics ranging from illegal immigration to marijuana.

The series focuses on three types of information: objective single-author narratives, opinion-based primary source quotations, and facts and statistics. The clearly written objective narratives provide context and reliable background information. Primary source quotes are carefully selected and cited, exposing the reader to differing points of view. And facts and statistics sections aid the reader in evaluating perspectives. Presenting these key types of information creates a richer, more balanced learning experience.

For better understanding and convenience, the series enhances information by organizing it into narrower topics and adding design features that make it easy for a reader to identify desired content. For example, in *Compact Research: Illegal Immigration*, a chapter covering the economic impact of illegal immigration has an objective narrative explaining the various ways the economy is impacted, a balanced section of numerous primary source quotes on the topic, followed by facts and full-color illustrations to encourage evaluation of contrasting perspectives.

The ancient Roman philosopher Lucius Annaeus Seneca wrote, "It is quality rather than quantity that matters." More than just a collection of content, the Compact Research series is simply committed to creating, finding, organizing, and presenting the most relevant and appropriate amount of information on a current topic in a user-friendly style that invites, intrigues, and fosters understanding.

Illegal Immigration at a Glance

Effects on Economy

Some studies suggest that illegal immigrants help the U.S. economy to grow by providing cheap labor, while other studies suggest that illegal workers depress wages and increase competition for low-skilled jobs.

Burden on Taxpayers

Large illegal immigrant populations in some states have dramatically increased social costs, especially for schools and emergency health services, but illegal immigrants also pay billions in taxes.

Assimilation Issues

Illegal immigrants tend to congregate with others who share their culture and language, causing some Americans to be concerned that they will not assimilate into U.S. culture.

U.S. Population Growth

The U.S. Census Bureau predicts that the U.S. population will double by the end of the century, largely because of immigration. Illegal immigrants make up a third of this fast-growing immigrant population.

Crime

Regions with large illegal immigrant populations report increases in serious crimes such as drug trafficking, human smuggling, prostitution, and gang activity.

Border Enforcement

Border fences, Border Patrol agents, and surveillance equipment deter illegal border crossings, but almost half of all illegal immigrants enter legally and then simply overstay their visas.

Targeting U.S. Employers

Current U.S. immigration laws prohibit employers from knowingly hiring illegal immigrants, but these laws have not been strongly enforced.

Amnesty for Illegal Immigrants

Amnesty would provide illegal workers in America with legal status and a path to U.S. citizenship, but past amnesty programs may have encouraged more illegal immigration.

Guest Worker Programs

Past guest worker programs have granted foreign workers the right to temporarily work in the United States, but temporary workers often stay and become illegal immigrants.

Overview: Illegal Immigrants in America

66 **The United States is currently undergoing the largest wave of immigration in over a century. But what makes this wave like no other is that so much of it is illegal.** 99

— Bob Simon, "IDs Sold to Illegal Immigrants," CBS News, April 20, 2005.

The United States is traditionally known as a nation of immigrants, a country founded on principles of tolerance for all people regardless of their race, color, religion, or country of origin. In some ways, this description is true: The United States has historically attracted immigrants from around the world and today is home to a wide variety of races and ethnicities. Gradual population growth followed the country's founding in the late 1700s; then, beginning in the 1880s, waves of immigrants totaling 27 million came to the United States from Europe. These late-nineteenth- and early-twentieth-century immigrants helped build America, providing labor for the country's rapid industrialization and helping the new nation push westward, settling towns from Ohio to California. Over time immigrants also added great diversity and richness to American culture, despite long periods of social disruption and assimilation.

Today America is once again experiencing a massive wave of immigration comparable to the migration from Europe more than a century ago. This time, however, an increasing number of immigrants are entering or staying in the United States illegally, a phenomenon that has now become the center of intense debate and disagreement.

Many illegal immigrants simply find an area of the border fence that is low or broken down, then they climb over it.

Today's Illegal Immigrant Wave

Today a total of 1 million to 1.5 million immigrants enter the United States each year. At least half, or up to 850,000, are believed to be illegal immigrants (also called illegal aliens or undocumented workers), a percentage that has risen steeply since the 1980s. According to the Pew Hispanic Center, a nonpartisan research organization, illegal immigration in the 1980s averaged about 130,000/year, rose to 450,000/year in the early 1990s, increased to around 750,000/year between 1995 and 1999, and has hovered at the 700,000–850,000/year level since about 2000. In fact, since the late 1990s more immigrants have come to the United States illegally than through legal processes. The exact numbers of illegal immigrants now living in the United States, however, is difficult to determine because illegal workers typically avoid responding to surveys or census questionnaires. Estimates range from 7 million to more than 20 million, but the most frequently cited statistic is the 2006 Pew Hispanic Center estimate of 12 million.

The vast majority of illegal immigrants, around 81 percent, are from Latin American countries. Mexicans make up more than half of all illegal immigrants—about 57 percent—and another 24 percent come mainly from Latin American countries, mainly those in Central America. According to Jeffrey Passel, a demographer with the Pew Hispanic Center, there are now about 11.6 million Mexican immigrants in the United States, and about 6.2 million are here illegally. Indeed, some reports say roughly 10 percent of the entire Mexican population of 107 million is now living in the United States. The rest of the illegal immigrants in America come from Asia (9 percent), Europe and Canada (6 percent), and Africa and other countries (4 percent).

The inflow of large numbers of Latin American immigrants is changing American demographics, causing Hispanics to become the fastest-growing minority group in the country. Unless the current trend of illegal immigration is slowed or halted, this illegal immigrant wave is expected to continue indefinitely, spiking the U.S. population dramatically.

The Beginning of Illegal Immigration

Today's high level of illegal immigration has its origins in the 1940s. Labor shortages caused by World War II prompted the U.S. government to set up a program to encourage Mexican laborers to enter the United States temporarily to work in agriculture, primarily in the American Southwest. Called the Bracero Program, this 1942 legislative scheme was the nation's first guest worker program. The program's goal was to import foreign workers—originally envisioned in the hundreds—only for temporary periods during the agricultural harvests and then encourage them to return home to Mexico when their labor was no longer needed.

Over the next twenty-one years, the Bracero Program brought about 4.8 million Mexican workers into the country and provided cheap labor to many U.S. employers. Although the program permitted the hiring of braceros only if a sufficient number of American workers could not be found, in reality U.S. employers often preferred the Mexican workers. These braceros were willing to work for lower wages than American workers and were less likely to join unions or otherwise press for better working conditions. The program was ended in 1964 during President John F. Kennedy's administration, largely as a result of complaints from labor unions and Mexican American groups that these foreign workers were taking jobs from Mexican American citizens and depressing their wages.

After the Bracero Program was terminated, however, many former braceros repeated their journey north for work, and many were hired by the same agricultural employers they had worked for earlier. As University of California sociologist Kitty Calavita explains, "A relationship of symbiosis between Mexican immigrants and U.S. employers had become entrenched."[1] A this point, however, these workers entered the country illegally. Although there is no way to know the exact number of ex-braceros who reentered illegally, the number of people caught trying to cross U.S. borders illegally grew rapidly from about 71,000 in 1960 to 345,000 by the end of that decade. The demand from U.S. businesses for cheap foreign workers has only grown since then, drawing what has now become a constant stream of illegal immigrants across the U.S.-Mexico border.

> " Congress responded to the public's desire for immigration reform by passing the 1986 Immigration Reform and Control Act (IRCA). "

The 1986 Immigration Reform and Control Act

This pattern of illegal immigration created by the Bracero Program, together with more liberal U.S. immigration policies adopted in the 1960s, ushered in a great post–World War II wave of immigration. Unlike the waves of immigrants from 1880–1920, immigrants came not from Europe but largely from Mexico, other parts of Latin America, and Asia. By the late 1980s immigration levels that had averaged about 178,000 annually during the early part of the century and were adding more than a million people each year to the U.S. population, about half of them illegal immigrants. Public opinion soon strongly favored legislative action to deal with the increasing number of illegal immigrants.

Congress responded to the public's desire for immigration reform by passing the 1986 Immigration Reform and Control Act (IRCA). This law was a compromise, an attempt to limit illegal immigration through increased enforcement combined with a program to legalize the millions of illegal workers already in the country.

On the enforcement side, IRCA became the first U.S. immigration law to provide for employer sanctions—that is, fines and possible criminal prosecution against employers who failed to verify an employee's eligibility to work in the United States or who "knowingly" hired illegal workers. Lawmakers rejected controversial verification schemes such as a national computer registry of all citizens' Social Security numbers in favor of a system that required employers to check for any two of a large group of identifying documents (including a driver's license and Social Security cards).

At the same time, IRCA included an amnesty provision that allowed millions of illegal immigrants already here to stay and apply for U.S. citizenship. The IRCA amnesty program legalized all illegal immigrants who had resided in America for 5 years as well as all illegal agricultural workers. This covered about 2.7 million people, or 60 percent of the approximately 4.5 million illegal immigrants believed to be living in the United States at the time. Because of this unprecedented favorable treatment of illegal immigrants, historian Reed Ueda has called IRCA "the most generous immigration law passed in U.S. history."[2]

Today, however, most experts agree that IRCA failed to limit illegal immigration. Employer sanctions in the law never really worked because of its unreliable verification system. Since employers were under no requirement to verify the accuracy of identification documents, the system encouraged illegal workers to simply present counterfeits, fostering a vast black market for fake Social Security cards and similar IDs. As economist Philip Martin has written, "The change in the farm labor market made by IRCA is the switch from undocumented workers to falsely documented workers."[3] In addition, even in cases where employers were found to be in violation, the federal government failed to enforce the law against the hiring of illegal workers. In 2004, for example, only three notices of intent to fine employers were issued by the U.S. Immigration and Customs Enforcement (ICE). This agency is part of the U.S. Department of Homeland Security. It replaced the U.S. Immigration and Naturalization Service, better known as the INS.

Many experts believe the IRCA amnesty program encouraged even more people to enter or stay in the United States illegally. First, because of lax enforcement, many illegal immigrants who did not qualify for amnesty nevertheless remained in the country. Thereafter, millions more immigrated illegally into America, some joining family members who had won amnesty and others hoping for another amnesty program. The result was a doubling of the number of illegal immigrants. As James Edwards Jr. of the Hudson Institute explains, "A lot of foreign lawbreakers got full amnesty, and it spurred a lot more mass illegal immigration. . . . The 2 million residual illegal alien population of 1988 grew to 3.5 million in 1990, 4 million in 1992, 5 million in 1996, 7 million in 2000 and [at least] 10 million today."[4]

Methods of Entry

About 50 to 60 percent of today's illegal immigrants enter the United States across the 2,000-mile-long U.S.-Mexico border, an impossibly long, open stretch of land, most of which is unfenced and difficult and costly to police or protect. As political scientist Samuel P. Huntington notes, "No other First World country has a land frontier with a Third World country—much less one of 2,000 miles."[5] The United States also shares a long northern border with Canada, but the Canadian border has not been the site of large-scale illegal crossings. According to the Pew Hispanic Center, only 6 percent of the illegal immigrants in the United States come from Canada and Europe combined. The U.S. Customs and Border Protection (CBP), including the well-known Border Patrol, is charged with on-the-ground day-to-day protection. A contingent of U.S. border agents tries to police both borders, focusing mainly on the southern region, but experts agree this effort is greatly understaffed and concentrated in large border cities such as San Diego, California, and El Paso, Texas.

> " Only 6 percent of the illegal immigrants in the United States come from Canada and Europe combined. "

As a result, each day hundreds of people slip illegally into the United States, most of them from Mexico and other Latin American countries such as El Salvador, Guatemala, Honduras, Colombia, Ecuador, and the Dominican Republic. Some of these immigrants are smuggled past customs agents in the back of cargo trucks; others easily walk across the border at unguarded sites or wade across the Rio Grande, the river that forms the border between Texas and Mexico. Since border enforcement was stepped up in certain urbanized parts of the southern border, however, more and more people risk their lives crossing at remote locations in the brutal deserts and mountains of Arizona and California. An increasing number of illegal immigrants also are reportedly using the services of expensive human smugglers, often called "coyotes," many of whom are associated with organized crime.

Crossing the border in any of these ways without a valid passport and U.S. visa is a misdemeanor for a first offense and a felony for subsequent violations. Immigrants who are caught illegally crossing the border by Border Patrol agents are usually fingerprinted and immediately returned to Mexico. If they are found to be repeat offenders or to have criminal records, however, they may be arrested and imprisoned.

Close to half, or between 40 to 50 percent, of all illegal immigrants now living in the country, however, do not enter illegally across U.S. borders. Instead, they are visa overstayers—people who enter the United States legally with temporary work, student, or tourist visas and then simply fail to return to their home countries when the visas expire. Finding out what countries these people come from is difficult because the government does not track the information. The largest number is believed to come from Asia—primarily India, China, the Philippines, and South Korea. Most overstayers tend to be more educated than illegal immigrants who cross the border illegally. As Allan Wernick, chairman of the Citizenship and Immigration Project at the City University of New York, says, "As a class, they're educated, skilled, and innovative."[6] The federal government historically has not closely monitored visa holders, but after the terrorist attacks of September 11, 2001, it began to check visa holders from countries with large populations known to be sympathetic to terrorists.

The Lure of Jobs

Regardless of how they get here, almost all illegal immigrants come to the United States to work and create a better life for themselves and their families. Indeed, the illegal population now makes up a significant part of the American workforce and economy. Although some work as professionals or attend school, the majority are poor, uneducated adults who work in menial jobs. Typically, illegal workers are employed at building sites as construction workers, in U.S. hotels as maids or service workers, in factories processing chickens or packing meat, on farms picking crops, or in restaurants working as cooks or dishwashers. Others work as gardeners, house cleaners, or nannies in private homes.

Such jobs, although low-paying by U.S. standards, often pay more than ten times the wages in poorer countries. As news editor Art Moore explains, "The average illegal worker can make about $60 a day in the U.S. compared to about $5 a day in Mexico."[7] The lure of U.S. jobs, therefore, is enhanced by high levels of unemployment and the widespread lack of decent-paying work in many of the immigrants' home countries.

Ironically, Mexico, the country that sends the most illegal immigrants to America, is a sizable country with abundant natural resources, a large economy, and a population only one-third that of the U.S. population. Yet despite these resources and this potential, Mexico historically has had a stagnant economy and a high poverty rate. In the regions that border the United States, for example, about 28 percent of Mexicans live in poverty. Most commentators attribute these problems to entrenched government corruption that often siphons off the country's wealth into private hands. In fact many critics claim that the Mexican government tacitly encourages the migration of its poor into the United States as an easy and effective way to ease Mexico's poverty. Immigration reduces the number of poor people in Mexico and also produces huge returns in the form of remittances—monies sent back to Mexico by immigrants working in the United States. According to *BusinessWeek Online* reporter Geri Smith, "An estimated 11 million Mexicans living in the U.S.—some legally and some illegally—. . . [sent] a record $20 billion to Mexico in 2005, a 20% increase over [2004]."[8]

> " Immigration [to the United States] reduces the number of poor people in Mexico. "

This remittance income, says writer John Mendez, "provides the Mexican economy with its second largest source of capital. Only oil generates more foreign reserves than remittance[s] from expatriates working in the USA."[9]

Putting Down Roots

The magnet of U.S. jobs, the porous border, the poverty in Mexico and other source countries, the hope for amnesty, and the lack of enforcement of U.S. immigration laws combine to produce massive illegal immigration into the United States. Once here, illegal immigrants settle throughout the country. California, however, has more illegal residents than any other state—approximately 2.4 million. It is estimated that the state absorbs about 73,000 illegal immigrants each year and that one of every 15 state residents is now an illegal immigrant. After California, the states with high illegal populations include Texas (1.4 million), Florida (850,000), and New York (650,000). Other states throughout the nation are also beginning to attract sizeable groups of illegal workers.

Many illegal immigrants live in households with family members who are U.S. citizens or legal residents. This suggests that people often enter the country illegally to be with family members who have gained legal residence or citizenship under normal immigration processes or in past amnesty programs. Some illegal entrants also apply for and eventually become citizens under the family reunification provisions of U.S. immigration laws. Immigration, therefore, appears to have a chain effect, in which people move to the United States, acquire legal status, and later bring in more family members, either legally or illegally.

These family connections also indicate that, despite their nonlegal status, most illegal immigrants are putting down roots in the United States. Although a few people travel back and forth between their home countries and America and some are new arrivals, the U.S. government estimates that as many as 7 million of the approximately 12 million illegal immigrants

On April 10, 2006, these people marched in opposition to proposed reform to immigration laws. On May 1 millions of immigrants nationwide protested these proposed reforms to existing immigration laws.

now in the United States have lived here for five years or longer. Another 3 million may have lived here between two and five years. Many illegal immigrant mothers also have babies while they are living in the United States. These babies are sometimes referred to negatively as "anchor babies" because, under the U.S. Constitution, they automatically become citizens by birth and can act as grounds for the legalization of their parents and other relatives under U.S. immigration laws.

The Illegal Immigration Debate

The presence of so many illegal immigrants in the United States, and their effect on America's economy and culture, has sparked a heated debate among the American public. In classrooms, town halls, coffeehouses, businesses, and legislative meeting rooms across the country, people from all walks of life—ordinary citizens, corporate leaders, immigration experts, and politicians—have begun to consider what changes today's illegal immigration wave might mean to America and what, if anything, should be done to slow or stop this trend.

Illegal immigrants themselves are also expressing their concerns. On May 1, 2006, several million people, most of them of Latino heritage and many of them believed to be illegal immigrants, staged marches and protests in cities across the United States in support of illegal immigrant workers' rights. Protesters demanded amnesty, a path to citizenship, and better wages and working conditions. Commentators say the marches stirred up feelings on all sides of the illegal immigration issue.

Indeed, the illegal immigration debate is a deeply emotional and divisive one for many Americans. On the one hand, illegal immigrants are perceived by most people as hard-working and deserving of a chance to succeed in America. At the same time, however, the majority of Americans believe that illegal immigration should be reduced. Divisions have also arisen over remedies, especially on the issues of how to secure the U.S.-Mexico border, better enforce immigration laws, and award or deny amnesty or some other legal status to the 12 million illegal immigrants already in the United States. Proposals for immigration reform were introduced in the U.S. Congress in 2006, but the House of Representatives and the Senate took such different approaches to the problem that no compromise was reached. The topic of illegal immigration, therefore, is expected to remain in the forefront of American politics.

Does Illegal Immigration Harm the U.S. Economy?

66 **The immigration debate has divided much of the nation into groups that believe either that illegal immigrants steal jobs and strain social services, or groups that contend nonresidents are valuable for taking on gritty, low-paying menial work. The truth is that both these things are true.** 99

—Steve Watson, *InfoWars*, December 7, 2005.

The issue of whether illegal immigrants help or harm the U.S. economy is one of the most important questions in the debate over illegal immigration. Studies and statistics can be found to support either conclusion. Some economists argue that the economy benefits because illegal workers provide cheap labor to keep many American businesses growing and profitable. Other experts, however, claim that the cost of such a plentiful pool of foreign workers is fewer opportunities and lower wages for poor, unskilled American citizens and higher social service costs for taxpayers. The answer to this question may depend largely on one's perspective: Some people and businesses clearly benefit from the labor of illegal immigrants but these benefits may come at the expense of other Americans.

Cheap Labor

It is undisputed that illegal immigrants are already a significant part of the U.S. economy. The Pew Hispanic Center estimates that as of 2005 illegal workers made up about 5 percent of the civilian U.S. workforce.

Other estimates are even higher, as much as 8 to 10 percent of the U.S. workforce. According to recent studies, most illegal immigrants are concentrated in just a few industries: hospitality industries such as hotels and restaurants (18 percent), construction (17 percent), manufacturing (16 percent), retail (12 percent), service industries such as landscaping and cleaning (6 percent), and agriculture (3 percent).

Illegal immigrants support the U.S. economy largely because they provide an economic benefit—namely, a willingness to work for low wages. As *San Francisco Chronicle* staff writer Carolyn Said has noted, "Immigrants provide a ready source of relatively cheap labor that keeps . . . business humming and elevates profits."[10] Businesses say these low labor costs help to keep prices low for U.S. consumers for basic goods such as food and housing. In a global economy, the free movement of cheap laborers also allows U.S. companies to compete with low-wage businesses abroad without moving their operations out of the country.

Economic Growth

The large influx of immigrants stimulates economic growth in another way by increasing the demand for products and services produced by American businesses. As Said explains, "More people means more consumers spending money on food, rent and a range of necessities and luxuries."[11] In fact, U.S. businesses are increasingly viewing the illegal population as a huge potential market for their goods and services. As *Business Week* reports, "Big U.S. consumer companies—banks, insurers, mortgage lenders, credit-card outfits, phone carriers, and others—have decided that a market of 11 million or so [illegal immigrant] potential customers is simply too big to ignore."[12]

> "The free movement of cheap laborers also allows U.S. companies to compete with low-wage businesses abroad."

Even economists who support reducing illegal immigration agree that the U.S. economy is growing faster due to the supply of illegal workers. Andrew Sum, the director of labor market studies at Northeastern University, for example, states, "We couldn't have grown nearly as much as we did in the '90s if we didn't have [illegal] immigrants. And in the last few years our growth would have been slower."[13] Many people even believe the U.S. economy is now dependent on this foreign workforce. As immigration lawyer Greg Siskind suggests, "If all these illegal immigrants disappeared from this country, the economy would collapse."[14]

Effects on American Workers

Even if illegal workers benefit certain parts of the U.S. economy, many experts believe a large supply of illegal immigrant workers depresses wages in the industries in which they are concentrated and creates unwanted competition for low-skilled, less-educated American workers. A common complaint is that American companies prefer illegal foreign workers who will not speak out against low pay or poor working conditions out of fear of deportation. Some say the current system of illegal foreign labor thus creates an underclass of workers that is underpaid and often not given the protections of U.S. labor law, such as minimum wages and overtime pay.

> **Many experts believe a large supply of illegal immigrant workers depresses wages.**

The expert evidence on this issue, however, is mixed. Donald Huddle, a Rice University economics professor, found in 1996 that illegal immigrants were displacing roughly 730,000 American workers every year, at a cost of about $4.3 billion a year in lost wages. Harvard economist George J. Borjas reached similar conclusions in a 2004 study; he found that by "increasing the supply of labor between 1980 and 2000, immigration reduced the average annual earnings of native-born men by an estimated $1,700, or roughly 4 percent."[15] According to Borjas, the economic principle is very simple: Increasing the supply of foreign workers, whether by legal or illegal immigration, creates a labor surplus that drives down wages in affected industries. Many of the workers harmed by illegal immigration, Borjas says, are poor Hispanic and black Americans who lack skills or a high school diploma.

Other experts downplay the effect of illegal immigration on American workers. University of California–Berkeley economist David Card, for example, has argued that the "evidence that immigrants have harmed the opportunities of less educated natives is scant."[16] Card acknowledges that wages for uneducated workers have dropped in some places with high populations of illegal immigrants, such as California, but he notes that other places with low numbers of illegal workers, such as Ohio, have seen similar wage drops. He concludes that any depressive effects on U.S. wages are very small and could be the result of other factors, such as technology advances or the loss of manufacturing jobs due to globalization.

Jobs Americans Reject

Employers often justify hiring illegal workers for service or laborer jobs because American citizens consider them demeaning and are no longer willing to do them. As John Gay, a lobbyist for the American Hotel and Lodging Association, laments, "The trend is [for American parents] to push our own children into college to be rocket scientists or computer programmers. But who is going to do these hard jobs?"[17]

The counterargument, however, is that more Americans might want to do these undesirable jobs if they paid higher wages, and employers might be forced to pay higher wages if they no longer had access to so many illegal immigrants. As public policy professor Daniel J.B. Mitchell asserts:

> Americans will work at jobs that are risky, dirty or unpleasant so long as they provide decent wages and working conditions, especially if employers also provide health insurance. Plenty of Americans now work in such jobs, from mining coal to picking up garbage. The difference is they are paid a decent wage and provided benefits for their labor.[18]

Although business interests warn that increasing wages would increase food and other prices, others disagree. Economist Philip Martin, for example, has shown that labor makes up only about 10 percent of the retail price of a head of lettuce or other fresh produce; he concludes that raising the wages of farm workers would thus have very little effect on consumers.

Instead, some experts see an opposite trend—employers increasingly hiring illegal workers for highly desirable jobs that once paid relatively

> **Illegal workers today are increasingly being hired in the construction trades.**

good wages to American workers. For example, although many people think of illegal immigrants as farm workers, illegal workers today are increasingly being hired in the construction trades, where critics say they are replacing American skilled tradespeople and depressing wages. Philip Martin argues that the home-building and rehabilitation industry is now dominated by financially strapped subcontractors who turn to illegal workers to lower their labor costs and produce low bids. As Maryland resident Britt Minshall explains, "The customer will always buy the $2,000 roof and not the $2,500 one."[19]

Burden on U.S. Taxpayers

Another hotly debated economic issue is whether illegal immigrants create a burden on American taxpayers by using more government benefits and services than they pay to the government in taxes. Few people dispute that illegal immigrants come to the United States to work: As Shikha Dalmia, a senior analyst at the Reason Foundation, puts it, "Immigrants aren't flocking to the United States to mooch off the government."[20]

Experts also agree that illegal immigrants pay billions in taxes each year into federal and state governments. Those who work as employees and give fake Social Security numbers have federal and state taxes automatically deducted from their paychecks; for those who are self-employed, the Internal Revenue Service in 1996 began issuing identification numbers to enable them to file federal taxes. The federal government's intake from illegal residents is significant and includes approximately $7 billion a year in Social Security taxes.

Some economic studies have shown, however, that tax gains from illegal immigrants are dwarfed by the costs to American taxpayers for social programs such as welfare, education, and health care. A 1996 study by Donald Huddle and a 1997 study by the National Research Council (NRC), a private research institution created by Congress as part of the National Academy of Sciences (NAS), estimated the total fiscal burden (taxes minus services) caused by illegal immigrants to be somewhere around $20 billion a year.

More recently, a 2004 study by the Federation for American Immigration Reform (FAIR) found that illegal immigrants alone cost the federal government $26.3 billion a year in services but pay only about $16 billion in taxes, creating a federal deficit (taxes minus services) of more than $10 billion annually. FAIR says some of the largest federal costs associated with illegal immigrants are for Medicaid (federally paid health care) and food assistance programs such as food stamps. Federal welfare reform laws in 1996 specifically banned illegal immigrants from receiving these federal benefits, but their American-born children, as citizens, are still eligible. Some illegal immigrants themselves may have qualified for these programs, too, because proof of citizenship has only been required since July 2006.

The social costs for illegal immigrants are even higher at the state level because states receive relatively little in the way of tax revenues from illegal populations but must shoulder most of their education and health costs. California, the state with the largest illegal immigrant population, has one of the highest tax burdens. FAIR estimates that illegal residents in that state create an annual fiscal deficit of about $9 billion, or approximately $1,183 per year in extra taxes for each native-born household.

Education Costs

One of the most significant impacts of illegal immigration appears to be on public schools. States with high numbers of illegal immigrants, such as California and Texas, complain that illegal populations are bankrupting public school systems and causing budget cuts that result in larger class sizes, teacher layoffs, shorter library hours, fewer extracurricular activities, and overall inferior education for all students. In California alone, according to a June 2005 report by FAIR, annual illegal immigrant education costs amounted to $7.7 billion, or 13 percent of the state's school budget. Overall, more than 15 percent of students in California schools are either illegal immigrants or the children of illegal immigrants. "When our government ignores and even encourages illegal immigration, a small number of employers end up with low-cost labor, while taxpayers end up with the bills and millions of children end up in schools drained of resources,"[21] argues Dan Stein, executive director of FAIR.

States face a terrible bind, however, because they are mandated by law to educate these children. In 1982 the U.S. Supreme Court, in *Plyler v. Doe,* ruled that illegal immigrant children are entitled to a free public education. In 1996 California voters approved Proposition 187 to deny public education to illegal immigrants, but the measure was later struck down as unconstitutional.

Health Care Costs

The illegal population is also draining funds from state health services, forcing some trauma centers and emergency rooms to close. Illegal immigrants are often destitute and without health insurance, and they flock to emergency rooms for health care because U.S. law forbids these facilities, both private and nonprofit, to refuse care to anyone because of inability to pay. In places with high concentrations of illegal immigrants, such as Los Angeles, California, many believe the situation has reached a crisis. As Fox News reports, "Sixty percent of [Los Angeles] county's uninsured patients are not U.S. citizens. More than half are here illegally. About 2 million undocumented aliens in Los Angeles County alone are crowding emergency rooms because they can't afford to see a doctor."[22]

> **Illegal immigrants are often destitute and without health insurance.**

Pro-immigrant groups counter that the contributions of illegal immigrants—the billions that they contribute to the federal government in Social Security and other taxes, and the sales taxes paid to states—help offset the costs they generate. Also, Standard & Poor's, a financial research and ratings company, has suggested that these costs for states and municipalities would not seem nearly as burdensome if the federal tax contributions of illegal workers could be earmarked to pay for the increased state and local expenditures.

And yet, the burden on state health services alone is so heavy that in May 2005 the U.S. government set aside $1 billion over four years to start paying hospitals and doctors for providing emergency care to illegal immigrants. California received the largest initial chunk of funds ($70.8 million), with the rest going to Texas, Arizona, New York, Illinois, Florida, and New Mexico. On balance, therefore, while illegal immigration may benefit the U.S. economy and treasury in some important ways, it also produces significant costs.

Does Illegal Immigration
Harm the U.S. Economy?

66 The costs of illegal immigration to the [U.S.] taxpayer are numerous, but the largest costs are education of their children, emergency medical care and incarceration for those arrested for crimes. 99

—Federation for American Immigration Reform, "What's Wrong with Illegal Immigration?" May 7, 2006. www.fairus.org.

Federation for American Immigration Reform is a national nonprofit public-interest organization dedicated to reforming the nation's immigration policies.

66 The May 1st [2006 protest] actions highlighted the economic importance of immigrant labor. Undocumented workers deserve legal status because of that labor—their inherent contribution to society. 99

—Nativo Lopez and David Bacon, "The Voices of Immigrants Must Be Heard," *Truthout/Perspective*, May 3, 2006. www.truthout.org.

Lopez is president of the Mexican-American Political Association and the Hermandad Nacional Mexicana, both immigrant rights organizations. Bacon is a California photojournalist and book author who documents labor, migration, and globalization issues.

* Editor's Note: While the definition of a primary source can be narrowly or broadly defined, for the purposes of Compact Research, a primary source consists of: 1) results of original research presented by an organization or researcher; 2) eyewitness accounts of events, personal experience, or work experience; 3) first-person editorials offering pundits' opinions; 4) government officials presenting political plans and/or policies; 5) representatives of organizations presenting testimony or policy.

66 The federal government's unwillingness to stem the tide of illegal immigrants has created billions in healthcare expenses. **99**

—Newt Gingrich and David Merritt, "Congress Should Pay for Immigrants' Healthcare," *Miami Herald*, May 6, 2005.

Gingrich is a former U.S. Speaker of the House and founder of the Center for Health Transformation. Merritt is project director for the Center for Health Transformation.

66 Illegal immigration is the number one reason our healthcare system is on life support. **99**

—Elton Gallegly, "Illegal Immigration Is Breaking the Healthcare System," March 2005, www.house.gov.

Gallegly is a member of the U.S. House of Representatives for California's Twenty-fourth District.

66 Illegal immigration into the United States is a highly profitable proposition for both employers and the US government, and it also benefits Mexico. **99**

—Deborah White, "Illegal Immigration Explained: Profits & Poverty, Social Security & Starvation," Liberal Politics: US, October 17, 2005. www.usliberals.about.com.

White is a writer and journalist specializing in liberal politics and progressive issues and perspectives.

66 Illegal immigration is not an economic gain to the vast majority of Americans. **99**

—Mark Wyland "Illegal Immigrants Don't Help Economy," *(San Diego) North County Times*, May 21, 2005.

Wyland is a state assemblyman for San Diego, California.

66 [The negative impact of illegal immigration on U.S. workers] is more than offset by the lower prices and wider range of goods and services that all workers enjoy because of immigration. 99

—Daniel T. Griswold, "The Need for Comprehensive Immigration Reform: Serving Our National Economy," testimony before the Senate Committee on the Judiciary, Subcommittee on Immigration, Border Security and Citizenship, May 26, 2005. www.cato.org.

Griswold is director of the Cato Institute's Center for Trade Policy Studies.

66 The economic and social consequences of illegal immigration across the 1,940 mile long America-Mexico border are staggering. 99

—Colorado Alliance for Immigration Reform, "Economic Costs of Legal and Illegal Immigration," 2006. www.cairco.org.

Colorado Alliance for Immigration Reform (CAIR) is a nonprofit organization concerned with America's rapid population growth and the devastating effects that growth will have on the future of Colorado and the nation.

66 Because they have few labor protections and are afraid to assert their rights, join [a union] organizing campaign, or complain about workplace conditions, undocumented workers endure low wages and poor working conditions. 99

—Michele Waslin, "Immigration Reform: Comprehensive Solutions for Complex Problems," National Council of La Raza, December 12, 2004. www.nclr.org.

Waslin is a senior policy analyst for National Council of La Raza, a Hispanic civil rights group.

66 **[The costs of illegal immigration] are disproportionately borne by low-income and minority Americans, while the benefits go to employers who prefer foreign to American labor.** 99

—Otis L. Graham Jr., *Unguarded Gates: A History of America's Immigration Crisis*. New York: Rowman & Littlefield, 2004, p. 181.

Graham Jr. is professor emeritus of history at the University of California, Santa Barbara, and the author and editor of several books.

66 **Much of the agricultural workforce [in California] is undocumented. Efforts have been made for years to get Americans to do the work, but they simply won't do it.** 99

—Dianne Feinstein, "The Immigration Debate: A Plan to Bring People Out of the Shadows," *San Francisco Chronicle*, April 2, 2006.

Feinstein is a U.S. senator from California.

66 **The U.S. does not have a shortage of workers; what we have is a shortage of employers willing to pay a living wage and maintain decent working conditions.** 99

—National Network for Immigrant and Refugee Rights, "National Statement to Support Human and Civil Rights for All Immigrants and to Oppose Compromise Immigration Reform Proposals: Fair and Just Immigration Reform for All," April 2006. www.nnirr.org.

National Network for Immigrant and Refugee Rights is a national immigrant rights organization composed of local coalitions and immigrant, refugee, community, religious, civil rights and labor organizations, and activists that seeks to expand the rights of all immigrants.

Does Illegal Immigration Harm the U.S. Economy?

- According to Bear-Stearns Asset Management, the total number of illegal immigrants in the United States may be as high as 20 million people.

- The U.S. Department of Homeland Security estimates that as of 2005 nearly 6 million Mexican illegal immigrants were living in the United States.

- The Pew Hispanic Center estimates that between 4.5 and 6 million of the illegal immigrants in the United States entered the country legally but did not leave when their visas expired.

- According to the Pew Hispanic Center, 94 percent of illegal male immigrants are employed; they make up one of every four drywall installers and landscape workers, one in five workers in meat and poultry packing, and one in six employees in the leisure and hospitality industry.

- A 2004 study by the Center for Immigration Studies found that the largest federal costs for illegal immigrants were for Medicaid ($2.5 billion); treatment for the uninsured ($2.2 billion); food assistance programs such as food stamps, WIC, and free school lunches ($1.9 billion); the federal prison and court systems ($1.6 billion); and federal aid to schools ($1.4 billion).

Illegal Immigrants Pay into Social Security Programs

This data represents payments into the Social Security program by workers who will not be able to claim the benefits because their card numbers do not match their names. Illegal immigrants are believed to make up the large majority of this group.

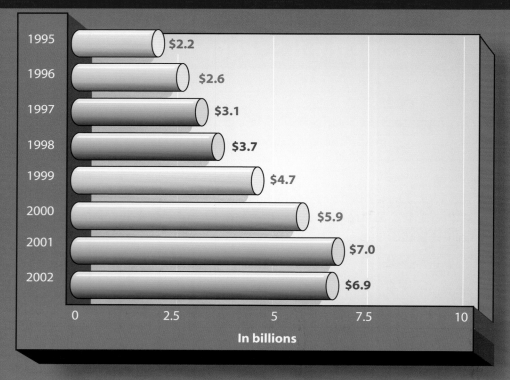

Year	Amount (in billions)
1995	$2.2
1996	$2.6
1997	$3.1
1998	$3.7
1999	$4.7
2000	$5.9
2001	$7.0
2002	$6.9

In billions

Source: Citizens for a Secure Border, "Effect on the Economy," 2006. www.citizensforasecureborder.org.

- Illegal immigrants provide cheap labor to many American industries. According to Kay Embrey of the Cornell Migrant Program, half of all farmworkers earn less than $7500 per year.

- The *Washington Post* reports that in 2005 California farmers faced a shortage of illegal workers to pick agricultural crops because workers are taking better-paying jobs in construction.

The U.S. Cost of Education for Illegal Immigrants (in millions of dollars)

This table lists the costs by state of education for illegal immigrants and their U.S.-born children. California, Texas, and New York account for over 50 percent of the total U.S. cost for educating illegal immigrants and their U.S.-born children.

State	Illegal Immigrants Students	U.S.-Born Children of Illegal Immigrants	Total
California	3,220.2	4,508.3	7,728.5
Texas	1,645.4	2,303.6	3,949.0
New York	1,306.3	1,828.9	3,135.2
Illinois	834.0	1,167.6	2,001.7
New Jersey	620.2	868.2	1,488.4
Florida	518.1	725.3	1,243.4
Georgia	396.7	555.3	952.0
North Carolina	321.3	449.8	771.1
Arizona	311.8	436.5	748.3
Colorado	235.0	329.1	564.1
Washington	228.9	320.5	549.4
Massachusetts	206.0	288.5	494.5
Virginia	188.7	264.2	452.9
Oregon	167.4	234.4	401.8
Michigan	135.4	189.5	324.9
Nevada	133.8	187.3	321.1
Maryland	117.0	163.8	280.8
Minnesota	115.2	161.3	276.6
Pennsylvania	99.9	139.9	239.8
Connecticut	95.2	133.3	228.5
Indiana	85.9	120.3	206.2
Wisconsin	83.9	117.5	201.4
Kansas	80.2	112.3	192.5
Utah	76.8	107.6	184.4
Ohio	76.3	106.9	183.2
Oklahoma	67.1	94.0	161.1
Tennessee	65.0	91.0	156.0
New Mexico	63.8	89.3	153.1
South Carolina	59.8	83.7	143.5
Nebraska	43.4	60.7	104.1
Iowa	41.3	57.8	99.1
Arkansas	37.3	52.2	89.5
Missouri	36.8	51.5	88.3
Rhode Island	36.4	51.0	87.4
Alabama	34.4	48.1	82.5
Idaho	27.3	38.2	65.5
Delaware	22.4	31.4	53.8
Kentucky	21.5	30.1	51.6
DC	19.6	27.5	47.1
Other States*	12.4	17.4	29.8
Alaska	11.3	15.8	27.1
Mississippi	9.9	13.8	23.7
Louisiana	7.3	10.2	17.5
Hawaii	3.0	4.2	7.2
	$11,919.9	$16,687.9	$28,607.8

* Other states include Maine, Montana, New Hampshire, North Dakota, South Dakota, Vermont, West Virginia, and Wyoming.

Source: Federation for American Immigration Reform, "Breaking the Piggy Bank,," 2004. www.fairus.org.

- A 2006 report by the Brookings Institution indicates that U.S. banks and other   businesses are increasingly accepting nontraditional forms of identification to offer services such as bank accounts, home loans, and cell phones to illegal immigrants.

- As reported by the *New York Times* in 2005, illegal workers contribute approximately $7 billion in Social Security tax revenue and about $1.5 billion in Medicare taxes each year.

Illegal Immigration and Health Insurance (percent without health insurance)

Illegal immigrants are much more likely to not have health insurance. The cost of caring for illegal immigrants is a major concern for hospitals, insurers, and the government.

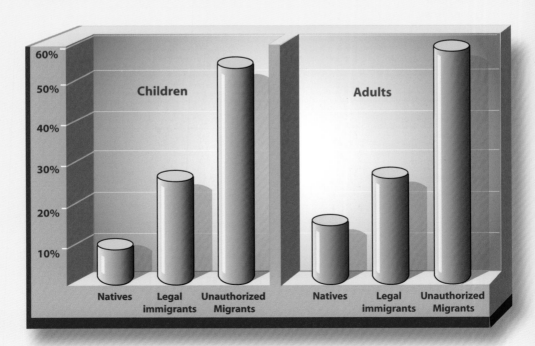

Source: Pew Hispanic Center, 2004. http://pewhispanic.org.

- The Federation for American Immigration Reform (FAIR) estimated in 2004 that between 287,000 and 363,000 children are born on U.S. soil to illegal aliens each year.

- According to the California Healthcare Association, Los Angeles County alone has reported spending $350 million a year on health care treatment for illegal immigrants.

- The Associated Press reported in 2005 that illegal immigrants are gaining a larger share of the job market and settling beyond traditional destinations such as California, and going to Illinois, New Jersey, Pennsylvania, Utah, Washington, Tennessee, Georgia, and the Dakotas.

- Illegal immigrants often are subjected to hazardous jobs and working conditions. A 2004 Associated Press investigation found that Mexican workers are 80 percent more likely to die on the job than are native-born American workers.

Does Illegal Immigration Threaten American Society?

66 Illegal immigrants contribute to dramatic changes in the racial, ethnic, and cultural composition of the country. **99**

—*Close Up Foundation*, "U.S. Immigration Policy," 2005. www.closeup.org.

A second important issue in the debate over illegal immigration is whether today's large numbers of illegal immigrants will strengthen American society or harm it. On the one hand, the United States has always been portrayed as an open and tolerant nation; indeed, the plaque at the base of one of the main symbols of America—the Statue of Liberty in New York Harbor—celebrates the nation's embrace of immigrants in the famous lines: "Give me your tired, your poor, your huddled masses yearning to breathe free. . . ."[23] On traditional humanitarian grounds, therefore, many Americans want to help illegal immigrants and urge the country to welcome them with open arms. On the other hand, according to many recent polls, a clear majority of Americans want to see illegal immigration reduced. Many people fear that the large numbers of illegal immigrants will erode traditional American values and culture or bring other negative changes to American society.

Assimilation into America

One concern is that today's illegal immigrants are failing to assimilate into American culture. Although new immigrants historically have faced enormous difficulties integrating into U.S. society, most of America's early immigrants eventually were assimilated. However, the last period of large-scale immigration from Europe was followed by decades of low immigration, a period that allowed the new immigrants to establish themselves and assimilate slowly. In contrast, an almost continuous and ever-increasing flow of illegal immigrants has traveled to the United States since the 1960s with almost no time to adjust to American culture. This constant influx of new immigrants makes it more difficult for new arrivals to integrate into American culture. Instead, many illegal immigrants settle into communities where they are surrounded by other new immigrants and separated from the rest of America. In addition, because of modern technologies like telephones, television, and the Internet, today's immigrants find it easier to maintain close relationships with family members and friends in their home countries—ties that may make them less compelled to form new connections in America.

> **Most of America's early immigrants eventually were assimilated.**

Critics see these as troubling signs that today's illegal newcomers may never embrace American language and culture. They worry that the illegal population may be destroying the traditional idea of America as a "melting pot," in which immigrant groups are expected to assimilate into the dominant American culture, and producing more of a "salad bowl" where each separate ethnic group instead tries to hold on to its distinct cultural identity. Such a result, some experts predict, could mean less social cohesion and an America that is splintered along racial and cultural lines.

Harvard political scientist Samuel P. Huntington is the most well known proponent of this view. He believes that the

> Persistent inflow of Hispanic immigrants threatens to divide the United States into two peoples, two cultures, and two languages. . . . Unlike past immigrant groups, Mexicans and other Latinos have not assimilated into mainstream U.S. culture, forming instead their own political and linguistic enclaves—from Los Angeles to Miami . . . and rejecting the Anglo-Protestant values that built the American dream.

Marcelo Suarez-Orozco, cofounder of the Harvard Immigration Project, however, disagrees with Huntington's view and says that Hispanic immigrants, both legal and illegal, are rapidly assimilating. He argues: "Huntington's views are not empirically based. Hispanics are learning English faster than did Italian and Polish immigrants a century ago, and 30 percent of adults from various first-generation Hispanic immigrant groups are marrying non-Latinos."[24]

Demographic Changes

In addition, because today's illegal immigrants are overwhelmingly from Mexico and Central America, they are contributing to a major demographic shift that is changing the face of America. Largely because of the concentrated Latino influx of illegal immigrants, Hispanics now outnumber blacks as the country's largest minority. In California, Texas, and New Mexico, states with large illegal immigrant populations, the numbers of Hispanics have grown so fast that non-Hispanic whites no longer form the majority. Demographers say a similar trend is occurring in many of America's largest cities.

These demographic changes cannot help but bring major changes to American culture, some positive and others potentially disruptive. Some commentators, for example, applaud the value of multiculturalism and point out the many ways Latino immigrants are enriching America. As *National Geographic* reporter A.R. Williams has noted, Latino immigrants, both legal and illegal, are "adding new tastes, sounds, and traditions to mainstream America."[25] Changes in the balance of ethnicities caused by immigration, however, can also stir up anxieties among native Americans who feel that Latin newcomers threaten traditional American customs and values. In the small town of Williams, California, for example,

> " **Hispanics now outnumber blacks as the country's largest minority.** "

the population has shifted from three-quarters Anglo to nearly three-quarters Latino in just two decades. Some estimate that as many as 20 percent of the town's businesses now cater to Latino tastes. Spanish is increasingly spoken at the local fire department and the school calendar was changed to create a three-week vacation at Christmas to allow families to return to Mexico for the holidays.

Many Anglo residents resent the changes and have either moved or pulled their children out of the local school system. Longtime resident Linda Granzella describes an event at a Williams High School football game that caused her to take her daughter out of the local elementary school. She said that 80 percent of the people in the stadium, which included mostly Hispanic spectators, did not rise when the national anthem was played at the beginning of the game. Perplexed, she asked people why they did not stand. The response, she said, was that the United States was not their country. To Granzella and others this sort of thinking signals a loss of American culture.

Population Effects

In addition to changing demographics, illegal immigrants are helping to feed an exponential increase in the U.S. population. Without high immigration levels, sociologists predict the U.S. population would level off and stabilize in coming decades. If current levels of legal and illegal immigration continue, however, the U.S. Census Bureau projects that the U.S. population, now at around 290 million, will double by the end of this century.

Illegal immigration is a large contributor to this population explosion. The total immigrant population has increased 57 percent just since 1990 and illegal immigrants already make up more than a third of this immigrant population. The illegal immigrant population, however, is growing rapidly; in fact, almost half of all illegal immigrants have arrived just in the last two decades. After settling in America, illegal immigrants continue to spur population growth because birth rates among Latin American groups are higher than among non-Hispanic whites and non-Hispanic blacks. Illegal immigrants from Mexico and Latin America, for example, tend to be rural Catholics who traditionally produce large families.

Many people fear that such a major increase in the population will negatively affect the quality of life in the United States. Some environmentalists warn that rising population will devastate the environment. As SUSPS, a network of Sierra Club members, contends, "Twice as many people will mean twice as many houses, roads, schools, hospitals, and office buildings and twice as much sprawl, traffic, overcrowding and congestion. It will place twice the pressure on our dwindling natural resources. . . . The environmental consequences of this doubling will be significant."[26]

Other commentators believe the United States still has plenty of room to expand and needs young immigrants to offset an aging native population. Without immigrants, some say, U.S. fertility rates would decline and the population would age, eventually creating declining Social Security receipts, a falling tax base, and labor shortages. Many countries in Europe are facing such a scenario, but thanks to high immigration, America will not have a population deficit.

Increased Poverty

As they add to the population, illegal immigrants also appear to be contributing to increased poverty in the United States. Most illegal immigrants are low-skilled; at least half of all illegal adults do not have a high school education. A 2003 study found that 27 percent of adult illegal immigrants and 39 percent of illegal immigrant children live below federal poverty guidelines. The poverty levels of Mexican illegal immigrants are the highest. The Center for Immigration Studies (CIS), for example, estimates that 74.2 percent of all Mexican illegal immigrants in the United States live at or near the poverty level. Critics ask whether the United States should be allowing such large numbers of poor, needy people to add to America's social burdens.

> " The poverty levels of Mexican illegal immigrants are the highest. "

In addition, some observers worry that this growing poor population, together with a shrinking base of middle-class jobs, might exacerbate an already widening class divide in American society between rich and poor. America's large middle class, often seen as one of the country's most notable successes, could narrow considerably. Jack Martin, special projects director for FAIR, for example, argues that U.S. society is already becoming more like a developing country, with larger wage discrepancies, more barriers to class mobility, and an increase in the number of gated communities that separate the rich from the rest of society. Because of this effect, Martin says illegal immigration will have "significant effects on the way that our society will be in the future if we don't get control over it."[27]

An Influx of Crime

Evidence also suggests that the illegal influx is bringing with it increased levels of criminal and drug activity. While many illegal immigrants are law-abiding once they begin new lives in this country, some were convicted of crimes in their home countries and continue to engage in criminal activities in America. Many cities with large illegal immigrant populations report record increases in serious crimes such as drug trafficking, human smuggling rings, prostitution, and gang activity.

Gang activity, in particular, is exploding in the United States. Most prevalent are transnational Latin gangs, including one called Mara Salvatrucha. These gangs have been linked with serious crimes (such as human smuggling, robbery, rape, assault, and murder) and are made up mostly of illegal immigrants. As Heather MacDonald, a senior fellow at the Manhattan Institute, told Congress in 2005, "In Los Angeles, 95 percent of all outstanding warrants for homicide . . . target illegal aliens. . . . Mara Salvatrucha is predominantly or majority illegal. Police officers will tell you that it's basically 100 percent illegal."[28]

Another telling statistic is the number of illegal immigrants who are arrested or incarcerated in state and federal prisons in the United States. A 2005 study of illegal immigrants by the U.S. General Accounting Office (GAO) found that more than half had been arrested between two and ten times, and 12 percent of these arrests were for violent offenses such as murder, robbery, assault, and sex-related crimes. The GAO in 2004 estimated that illegal immigrants make up 27 percent of the U.S. federal prison population. Large numbers of illegal immigrants can also be found in state prisons and local jails. The largest numbers are in states that have been the top immigrant destinations: California, Arizona, Florida, Illinois, New Jersey, New York, and Texas.

Criminal activity by illegal immigrants makes communities unsafe and creates significant police, incarceration, and health care costs for governments and taxpayers. The federal government provides some funds to reimburse states for this added burden, but these amounts do not begin to cover the real expenditures. California, for example, reportedly spent $635 million in 2003 to incarcerate illegal immigrants in state prisons, but was only reimbursed for $77 million.

Terrorism Concerns

Following the terrorist attacks of September 11, 2001, concerns have grown that lack of immigration controls and enforcement allows terrorists easy entry into the United States. Terrorists can cross the long Mexico or Canada borders illegally or obtain entry by legal visas and then disappear into the population when the visas expire. Even if caught and ordered deported, most have ample opportunity to disappear before a scheduled court date that is mandated before deportation can occur. In 2001, the U.S. government admitted that it did not know the whereabouts of at least 314,000 illegal immigrants who already had been ordered deported.

> **Illegal immigrants have participated in terrorist attacks on America.**

Already, illegal immigrants have participated in terrorist attacks on America. As Steven Camarota of CIS explains, "[Illegal aliens have] taken part in almost every major attack on American soil perpetrated by Islamic terrorists, including the first attack on the World Trade Center, the Millennium plot, the plot to bomb the New York subway, and the attacks of 9/11."[29] In fact, four of the nineteen terrorists who participated in the 9/11 attack (Zacarias Moussaoui, Satam al Suqami, Nawaf al Hamzi, and Hani Hanjour) were illegal immigrants who overstayed their visas. Illegal immigration, therefore, appears to be producing at least some negative effects on American society.

Does Illegal Immigration Threaten American Society?

66 **We are admitting over one million mostly poor people [as legal and illegal immigrants] into our society every year—a society that is already challenged to deal with the poverty of its natives.** 99

—Federation for American Immigration Reform, "The Cost of Immigration," July 2003. www.fairus.org.

The Federation for American Immigration Reform is a national nonprofit public-interest membership organization of concerned citizens who share a common belief that U.S. immigration policies must be reformed to reduce immigration numbers.

66 **Let us not forget that these [illegal] immigrants are people who simply want a better life, just like our parents and grandparents, who all came to the United States in similar situations.** 99

—ImmigrationDebate.com. 2005.

ImmigrationDebate.com is a private Web site that supports open immigration laws that treat immigrants to the United States with respect and dignity. The site encourages comments from those who have different perspectives on immigration in the United States.

* Editor's Note: While the definition of a primary source can be narrowly or broadly defined, for the purposes of Compact Research, a primary source consists of: 1) results of original research presented by an organization or researcher; 2) eyewitness accounts of events, personal experience, or work experience; 3) first-person editorials offering pundits' opinions; 4) government officials presenting political plans and/or policies; 5) representatives of organizations presenting testimony or policy.

❝[Americans] have been rattled by the appearance in their communities—especially in small towns, rural and suburban areas—of [illegal immigrant] newcomers speaking a different language (Spanish) and living in separate enclaves.**❞**

—David S. Broder, *Washington Post*, June 25, 2006.

Broder is a Pulitzer Prize–winning journalist and is a columnist with the *Washington Post*.

❝There is no basis to allegations that Latinos refuse to join U.S. society.**❞**

—Rodolfo de la Garza, *Hispanics Today*, 2003: *Cultural Loyalties vs. Political Commitments: Latino Immigrants and American Politics*, New York: HACR Research Institute, 2003.

Garza is vice president of the Tomás Rivera Policy Institute at Columbia University, a U.S. Latino policy research organization.

❝America is no longer asked to give refuge to the poor, huddled masses but to allow itself to be overrun by them. . . . A common theme in the demonstrations and school walkouts [of May 2006] was the preponderance of Mexican flags. The irony of demanding American citizenship while holding aloft the flag of a foreign country was not lost on American viewers.**❞**

—Cinnamon Stillwell, "Illegal Immigration Reaches Critical Mass," *San Francisco Chronicle*, April 5, 2006. www.sfgate.com.

Stillwell is a San Francisco writer.

66Most Mexican migrants to the United States never intend to settle permanently north of the border.99

—Douglas S. Massey, "Five Myths About Immigration: Common Misconceptions Underlying U.S. Border-Enforcement Policy," *Immigration Policy in Focus*, vol. 4, no. 6, August 2005.

Massey is a professor of sociology at Princeton University and an adjunct professor of sociology at the University of Pennsylvania who writes frequently about the topic of immigration.

66A legal, safe, orderly migration policy with full respect to human rights and labor rights will benefit the security and prosperity of both of our nations.99

—Vicente Fox, speech given to the joint session of the California Legislature, May 25, 2006.

Fox is the former president of Mexico and supports an open U.S. immigration policy.

66American citizens are suffering desperately as a result of the [government's] failure to deter illegal entry or to stop this population and immigration explosion.99

—George Putnam, "One Reporter's Opinion—Immigration/Population Explosion," NewsMax.com, May 13, 2005. www.newsmax.com.

Putnam is a television news reporter from California.

66The United States cannot assimilate quickly millions of abject poor who live in apartheid communities.99

—Victor Davis Hanson, "Assimilation Is the Real Debate," Tribune Media Services, April 3, 2006. www.victorhanson.com.

Hanson is a professor at the University of California, Fresno, and a senior fellow at the Hoover Institution, a public policy think tank.

66 **Assimilation requires time and the right conditions. It cannot succeed if we constantly flood the country with new, poor [illegal] immigrants or embark on a vendetta against those already here.** 99

—Robert J. Samuelson, "Conspiracy Against Assimilation," *Washington Post*, April 20, 2006. www.washingtonpost.com.

Samuelson is a columnist for the *Washington Post*.

66 **Immigration [both legal and illegal] contributes to the growing disparity between the rich and the poor in this country and the shrinking of the middle class.** 99

—Federation for American Immigration Reform, "Lower Wages for American Workers," January 2005. www.fairus.org.

The Federation for American Immigration Reform is a national nonprofit public-interest membership organization of concerned citizens who share a common belief that U.S. immigration policies must be reformed to reduce immigration numbers.

66 **Many [illegal immigrants] come for opportunities that America provides . . . but others have a more sinister intent.** 99

—Rob Simmons, press release, June 25, 2006, www.simmons.house.gov.

Simmons, a former CIA officer, is a Republican member of the House of Representatives from Connecticut.

66 **Without enactment of comprehensive immigration reform . . . our nation's security will remain vulnerable.** 99

—John McCain, press release, May 25, 2006. www.mccain.senate.gov.

McCain is a Republican senator from Arizona and an active participant in U.S. immigration policy reform.

Facts and Illustrations

Does Illegal Immigration Threaten American Society?

- A Pew Hispanic Center survey of March 2006 found that 48 percent of Americans believe that immigrants, both legal and illegal, threaten traditional American customs and values.

- In an April 2006 telephone poll by Zogby International, 67 percent of all Americans polled agreed that "the time has come to reduce immigration so we can assimilate the immigrants already in the country."

- A June 2006 report by the Pew Hispanic Center found that a majority of U.S. Hispanics believe that immigrants should be required to speak English to become a part of American society.

- Surveys in Mexico by the Pew Hispanic Center in recent years indicate that about four out of ten adults in the Mexican population would migrate to the United States if they had the means and opportunity. Two out of ten said they would be willing to live and work in the United States illegally.

- According to a study released in 2005 by the Pew Hispanic Center, more than 40 percent of Nevada's foreign-born population is in the United States illegally.

- The FBI estimates that half of all gang members in Los Angeles are illegal immigrants from Mexico or other parts of Latin America.

Illegal Immigrant Population Growth Accelerating

As these graphs show, the illegal immigrant population growth is accelerating in the United States. The decline in total immigrants from 1986–1989 was due to the 1986 Immigration Reform and Control Act that granted amnesty to millions of illegal immigrants living in the United States at the time.

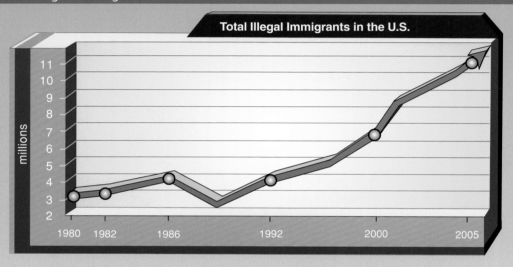

Total Illegal Immigrants in the U.S.

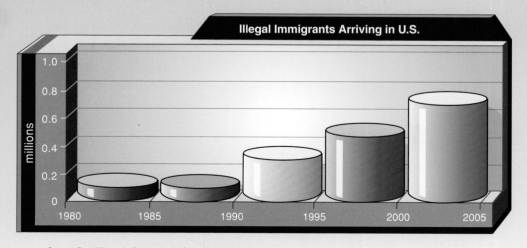

Illegal Immigrants Arriving in U.S.

Source: Pew Hispanic Center, 2006. http://pewhispanic.org.

Where Are Illegal Immigrants From?

In 2004 the majority of illegal immigrants in the United States were from Mexico. Less than 4 percent came from Africa.

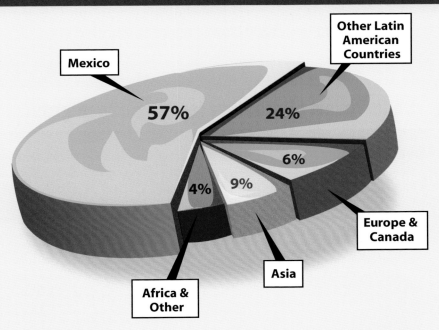

Mexico — 57%
Other Latin American Countries — 24%
Europe & Canada — 6%
Asia — 9%
Africa & Other — 4%

Source: Pew Hispanic Center, 2005. http://pewhispanic.org.

- An April 2005 study by the Government Accounting Office (GAO) found that the number of criminal aliens incarcerated in federal facilities at the end of calendar year 2004 was 49,000, an increase of 15 percent since 2001.

- A 2005 *New York Times* article states that 80,000 to 100,000 illegal immigrants who have been convicted of serious crimes are now living in the United States.

- Local police usually consider illegal immigration a matter for federal immigration authorities, and several American cities (Los Angeles, Chicago, Seattle, San Francisco, and New York City) have laws prohibiting police from asking criminal suspects about their immigration status.

- Out of twelve al Qaeda operatives who took part in anti-U.S. terrorism between 1993 and 2001, seven were visa overstayers.

Child Poverty Rate High for Illegal Immigrants

The chart below shows that children of illegal immigrants are much more likely than children of lawful immigrants to live in poverty. More than 1 out of 3 children of illegal immigrants lives in poverty compared with 1 out of 5 for legal immigrants and 1 out of 10 for whites.

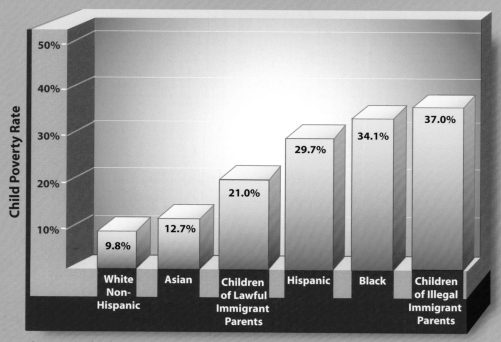

Source: National Vital Statistics; Pew Hispanic Center; U.S. Department of Health and Human Services; U.S. Census Bureau; National Center for Health Statistics, 2003.

Illegal Immigrants and Crime

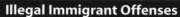

Illegal Immigrant Offenses

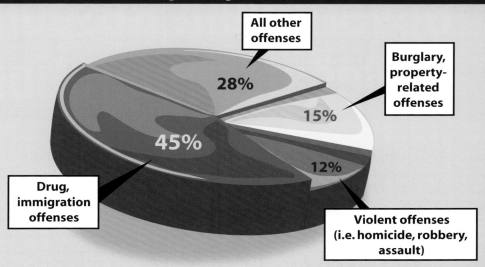

All other offenses
28%

Burglary, property-related offenses
15%

Drug, immigration offenses
45%

Violent offenses (i.e. homicide, robbery, assault)
12%

Illegal Immigrant Offenses by State

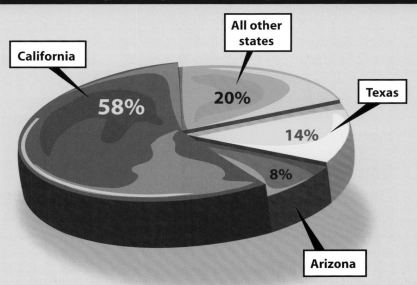

California
58%

All other states
20%

Texas
14%

Arizona
8%

The data above are based on a sample of 55,000 illegal immigrants who had been incarcerated in federal or state prisons for criminal offenses. Eighty percent of all crimes were committed in California, Texas, or Arizona.

Source: U.S. Department of Justice; Government Accounting Office, 2005.

How Should the Government Respond to Illegal Immigration?

> 66 **While most people share the goal of reducing illegal immigration, most do not agree on what to do about it.** 99

—Esther Pan, "The U.S. Immigration Debate," Council on Foreign Relations, March 22, 2006.

Immigration has historically been a contentious policy issue for Americans and today's debate about illegal immigration is particularly intense. Polls show most Americans are in favor of strong punitive measures to prevent and/or reduce illegal immigration. According to a June 2006 CNN poll, for example, 60 percent of Americans favor imposing large fines on employers who hire illegal aliens and 78 percent approve of placing more Border Patrol and federal law enforcement officers along the U.S.-Mexico border. Despite this public support for stopping illegal immigration, however, many employers, a variety of special interests, and a number of politicians oppose stronger immigration enforcement. As a result, no clear official consensus has emerged for responding to the illegal immigrant flow.

Border Security

Many proposals for dealing with illegal immigration focus on strengthening the security of the U.S.-Mexican border. Existing border enforcement is very weak despite recent increases in the numbers of border agents. As *Washington Post* columnist David S. Broder explains, "The size of the Border Patrol has grown by 3,000—from 9,000 to 12,000—in recent years and spending on border security has gone up at an even faster pace. But the tide of illegal immigrants . . . still floods into the United States."[30]

The U.S. House of Representatives responded to these concerns about border security in December 2005 by passing the Border Protection, Antiterrorism, and Illegal Immigration Control Act (H.R. 4437). The centerpiece of the bill's border security scheme was a plan to build a fence along 700 miles, or roughly one-third, of the U.S.-Mexico border. The fence would actually be a double set of 15-foot-high steel mesh walls equipped with floodlights, surveillance cameras, and motion detectors. It would be built in 5 border areas that now experience the most illegal crossings. The Senate, too, called for improving border fences in its Comprehensive Immigration Reform Act (S. 2611), passed in May 2006, but this act provided for only 340 miles of additional border fencing.

Existing border enforcement is very weak.

More Fences

Supporters say improved fences will show that the United States is serious about stopping illegal immigration and provide much-needed support to beleaguered border agents. As Joe Kasper, a spokesperson for San Diego Republican representative Duncan Hunter, explained, "The fence in itself is a force multiplier. . . . It allows Border Patrol agents to refocus their attention to other areas because it won't require as many Border Patrol agents to monitor a location as it would without a fence."[31]

Fence proposals, however, also generated strong opposition. The House bill was the impetus for the massive immigrant rights demonstrations of April 2006. Many protesters saw the fence proposal as a militarization of the border, a policy they say is incompatible with friendly U.S.-Mexico relations and America's history as a welcoming nation. Other critics of the fence proposal questioned the price tag of such a huge construction project (at least $2.2 billion), and some worried that the barriers would block migration paths of wildlife and damage desert ecosystems. Such a long fence also could take years to build; a fourteen-mile-long fence has been under construction in San Diego since 1996, stalled by environmental and legal challenges.

Another concern was that a more fortified fence in parts of the border might simply shift illegal border crossings to other, more treacherous areas without diminishing the total number of border crossings. In areas such as San Diego, where the government has already upgraded fencing, illegal immigrants simply shifted eastward to more remote and dangerous routes through the treacherous mountains and hot deserts of California and Arizona. This has resulted in a large increase in the number of illegal immigrant deaths; in 2005, the Border Patrol estimated that 473 people died trying to enter the United States illegally.

Despite these concerns, the Senate in September 2006 gave final approval to the Secure Fence Act, legislation that had already passed the House of Representatives. This legislation provided for 700 miles of additional fencing along the United States-Mexico border.

Added Manpower and Technology

Other commentators have stressed the need for more border agents and technology, such as night-vision cameras, motion detectors, helicopters, and unmanned aerial drones. Some critics say the billions required to build a 700-mile fence could fund 2,500 new Border Patrol agents for up to 5 years—a 22 percent increase—or be more wisely spent on other types of security enhancements.

In May 2006 President George W. Bush acted on this idea by proposing a 50 percent increase in the number of Border Patrol agents, from 12,000 to 18,000 by the end of 2008. Bush's plan also called for more high-tech surveillance devices, increased funding for state and local law enforcement in border states, and the deployment of 6,000 National Guard troops to help police the Mexico border until more border agents could be added. The Senate bill largely endorsed Bush's proposals but called for 14,000 additional border agents by 2011.

Many experts believe, however, that such a long border can never really be completely closed because it would take an unrealistic level of manpower to patrol the entire border area. As analyst Jorge Chabat explains, "For decades, each president has increased police forces on the border and the number of migrants has increased, not declined. . . . A border that's closed completely? It's fantasy."[32]

Moreover, experts point out that the various border security proposals will have no effect on visa overstayers who enter the country legally and then become illegal when their visas expire. Although this problem has not attracted as much media attention as the issue of border crossings, overstayers make up almost half of the illegal immigrant population and are also a potential terrorist threat. CIS director Mark Krikorian asserts, "Any serious effort to foil terrorist attacks on the United States must have as a centerpiece the prevention and removal of overstays."[33] For these reasons, other enforcement proposals have been gaining increasing support.

Targeting Employers

Many immigration experts believe that the key to reducing illegal immigration is better enforcement of U.S. immigration laws that target employers who hire illegal workers. As Maria Echaveste, an immigration expert at the Center for American Progress, explains, "So long as . . . we are not serious about cracking down on employers who hire undocumented workers, people will seek to come in."[34] Existing immigration law already makes it unlawful for employers to knowingly hire illegal immigrants or to hire anyone without complying with verification procedures. These procedures currently require employers to inspect applicants' identification documents to verify that workers are citizens or legal residents, and then document this action by completing the Employment Eligibility Form, commonly known as the I-9 form.

> **Procedures currently require employers to inspect applicants' identification documents.**

Critics say, however, that federal immigration authorities do very little to check I-9 forms. In addition, many people argue the existing verification system is weak because it doesn't require employers to double-check IDs that appear genuine on their face. In fact, current law includes an antidiscrimination provision that may discourage employers from questioning documentation, for fear that they might be seen as discriminating against Latino citizens or other ethnic groups. As a result illegal immigrants simply purchase fake IDs and use them to get jobs in the United States.

Experts have proposed solutions to these problems. First, they say, employers need a simple way to truly verify immigration status. They need either a tamper-proof national ID card or a national computer registry that employers could call to check an applicant's immigration status. Other recommendations for a new employer-sanctions program include raising the fines on employers who violate the law, from the current maximum of $11,000 per illegal alien to as much as $20,000 to $40,000. Supporters say these ideas would help reduce the numbers of illegal immigrants, both illegal entrants and overstayers, without massive deportations. Instead, as immigration expert James Edwards Jr. explains, improved employer enforcement would cause "a gradual decrease of the illegal alien population by attrition,"[35] since many illegal immigrants unable to find jobs will voluntarily decide to leave the country.

In 2004 Congress authorized a program called Basic Pilot to test a computer verification system in all fifty states. The program allows employers, on a voluntary basis, to check applicants' employment status by keying data into a Department of Homeland Security (DHS) Web site. DHS then checks the information against Social Security and immigration records and provides verification to the employer, usually within 24 hours. The program has so far been used by 6,200 employers at 25,000 hiring sites. Although some have criticized inaccuracies in the federal government databases, both the House and Senate have proposed implementing this type of a verification system on a mandatory basis, phasing it in slowly to give employers time to adopt it.

Opposition to Employer Sanctions

Americans are solidly behind employer sanctions, but strong opposition comes from all sides of the political spectrum. Business lobbyists, for example, have long criticized any form of employer sanctions, arguing that they disrupt the ability to do business, hurt the economy, and place private companies in the inappropriate position of policing immigration on behalf of the government. Employers also oppose proposals for a better employee verification system, saying it would force them to deal with bureaucratic agencies and federal databases that are often inaccurate. As photojournalist David Bacon explains, "The Social Security Administration [SSA] would become immigration police . . . and would require employers to fire anyone whose documents they question. The current Basic Pilot program, which moves in this direction, has shown the SSA database to be rife with errors."[36]

Immigrant rights groups and unions, meanwhile, argue that employer sanctions allow employers to exploit illegal immigrants. As Sasha Khokha, communications director for the National Network for Immigrant and Refugee Rights (NNIRR), explains: "[Existing employer] sanctions gave employers a tool to silence workers. Many workers unable to show documentation endure harsh working conditions, knowing that finding another job will be difficult without authorization. Employers facing a union organizing drive frequently threaten to call the INS 'on themselves,' knowing that an INS raid will have a chilling effect."[37] Employer verification programs, advocates say, may also produce discrimination against Latinos. Employers might simply refuse to hire all Latinos in order to avoid delays and verification problems that may be associated with illegal applicants. For these reasons, longtime labor organizer Eddie Canales says, "Employer sanctions are really employee sanctions."[38]

> **Employer verification programs . . . may also produce discrimination against Latinos.**

In addition, critics such as the American Civil Liberties Union (ACLU) have long opposed computer-based verification proposals as a threat the privacy of workers and charge that they could lead to warrantless government data searches, a national worker blacklist, and identity theft. As ACLU legislative counsel Gregory T. Nojeim has cautioned, "A national data base and ID system raises grave concerns about invasions of privacy and personal freedom. . . . Moreover, no system can be entirely free from abuse—even the Pentagon's files have been accessed without authorization."[39]

Guest Worker Programs

Yet another approach to illegal immigration, supported largely by business, is a guest worker program that would grant temporary work status to foreign workers. Advocates claim that such a program would address the labor needs of the U.S. economy by legitimizing a massive workforce that is already present in the United States and at the same time help reduce illegal entries. As Migration Policy Institute analyst Deborah Meyers argues, "There needs to be a legal mechanism for people to enter and work in temporary jobs. . . . If there are legal channels of entry, why in the world would you risk your life to enter illegally?"[40] Bush has embraced the guest worker approach, and the 2006 Senate bill included a guest worker provision that would allow up to 200,000 workers into the country on temporary, six-year work visas.

Past guest worker programs, however, have not decreased illegal immigration. Rather, once here, most guest workers typically want to stay in the United States permanently, contributing to increased illegal immigration. As immigration experts Philip Martin and Michael Teitelbaum argue, "Far from mitigating illegal immigration, the . . . last major temporary worker program [the Bracero Program] actually initiated and accelerated its flow."[41] Because the 2006 Senate proposal allows temporary workers to eventually transition to permanent status and citizenship, it virtually ensures that most recipients would remain in America. For this reason, many people see current guest worker proposals as a form of amnesty.

Guest worker programs also have long been criticized by labor and immigrant groups for exploiting vulnerable foreign workers, driving down wages and working conditions, and helping to break union organizing efforts. Because of these wide differences of opinion about the solutions for illegal immigration, legislators have so far failed to find a compromise.

How Should the Government Respond to Illegal Immigration?

66 **For decades, the United States has not been in complete control of its borders. As a result, many who want to work in our economy have been able to sneak across our border, and millions have stayed.** 99

—President George W. Bush, televised address to the nation on immigration reform, May 15, 2006. www.whitehouse.gov.

Bush is the forty-third president of the United States.

....

66 **Mexico believes that it will take more than just enforcement or building walls to truly solve the challenges caused by the immigration phenomenon.** 99

—Vicente Fox, speech given to the joint session of the California Legislature, May 25, 2006.

Fox is the former president of Mexico and supports an open U.S. immigration policy.

....

66 **What America needs is not closed borders or open borders, but smart borders.** 99

—Edward Kennedy, press release, November 25, 2005, www.kennedy.senate.gov.

Kennedy is a Democratic senator from Massachusetts and has worked with Senator McCain of Arizona on immigration legislation.

....

* Editor's Note: While the definition of a primary source can be narrowly or broadly defined, for the purposes of Compact Research, a primary source consists of: 1) results of original research presented by an organization or researcher; 2) eyewitness accounts of events, personal experience, or work experience; 3) first-person editorials offering pundits' opinions; 4) government officials presenting political plans and/or policies; 5) representatives of organizations presenting testimony or policy.

"A secure, state-of-the-art border fence must be one element of any comprehensive effort to address the illegal immigration problem. Similar fences in Israel have reduced terrorist attacks by up to 95%."

—Let Freedom Ring, Inc., "Immigration Is Out of Control," WeNeedAFence.com, 2005. www.weneedafence.com.

Let Freedom Ring is a public nonprofit policy group that promotes constitutional government, economic freedom, and traditional values.

"Because enforcement has increased the danger and cost of crossing the border, many of those who come in now stay longer."

—Hans P. Johnson, "At Issue: Illegal Immigration," Public Policy Institute of California, 2006. www.ppic.org.

Johnson is an economist with the Public Policy Institute of California, a privately funded research organization dedicated to improving public policy in California.

"By requiring businesses to verify the legal status of their employees, we can both reduce the current illegal alien population and discourage future illegal immigration."

—Tom Tancredo, press release, 2006. www.tancredo.org.

Tancredo is a member of the House of Representatives for the Sixth District of Colorado.

"The current system of employer sanctions has failed to deter undocumented workers from coming to our country. Instead, it has fostered discrimination against minorities and exploitation of immigrant workers."

—United Auto Workers, "Immigration," 2006. www.uaw.org.

The United Auto Workers (UAW) is a nationwide union that represents workers in the automobile industry.

66It's an unspoken agreement . . . [that] the [illegal] employee provides acceptable ID that appears authentic, the employer asks no questions, and the US government looks the other way.99

—Deborah White, "Illegal Immigration Explained—Profits & Poverty, Social Security & Starvation," About.com, May 19, 2006. www.usliberals.about.com.

White is a writer and journalist specializing in liberal politics and progressive issues and perspectives.

66Should you actually want to stop Mexicans . . . from coming to the United States, here is how to do it: Find an illegal worker at a large corporation . . . then put the CEO of that corporation in prison for two or more years for violating the law against hiring illegal workers.99

—Molly Ivins, "Molly Ivins: Immigration 101," CNN.com, March 30, 2006. www.cnn.com.

Ivins is an author and nationally syndicated columnist from Texas.

66We need to establish a temporary worker program that permits workers from other countries . . . to fill jobs that would otherwise go unfilled.99

—John McCain, press release, March 30, 2006. www.mccain.senate.gov.

McCain is a Republican senator from Arizona and an active participant in U.S. immigration policy reform.

66Guest worker programs are a bad idea and harm all workers.99

—John Sweeney, press release, March 28, 2006. www.afl-cio.org.

Sweeney is president of the AFL-CIO, a national organization committed to workers' rights and bringing economic justice to the workplace.

66 **Authorities—from the White House down—need to make an unambiguous commitment to immigration [law] enforcement.** 99

—Mark Krikorian, "Downsizing Illegal Immigration," May 2005. www.cis.org.

Krikorian is the executive director of the Center for Immigration Studies.

66 **One side of the political aisle seems too eager to cater to illegal immigrants and their families for votes, while the other wants to exploit them for cheap labor.** 99

—Jon E. Dougherty, *Illegals: The Imminent Threat Posed by Our Unsecured U.S.-Mexico Border*. Nashville, TN: WND Books, 2004, p. 9.

Dougherty is a paramedic and corpsman for the U.S. Naval Reserve and Marine Corps who now works as an investigative reporter and author.

How Should the Government Respond to Illegal Immigration?

- In a June 2006 CNN poll, 67 percent of Americans polled said they wanted to see illegal immigration decreased.

- According to a 2004 *Time* magazine article, more than 4,000 illegal immigrants walk into the United States each day across the 375-mile-long border between Arizona and Mexico.

- The Immigration Forum estimates that building a fence along the entire U.S.-Mexico border would cost about $9 billion—about $2.5 billion more than the total U.S. Immigration and Customs Enforcement (ICE) budget for fiscal year 2005.

- According to the U.S. Border Patrol, between January 1995 and March 2004 more than 2,640 illegal immigrants died while trying to cross the U.S.-Mexico border, and another 473 migrants lost their lives in 2005.

- Political commentator David Broder has reported that over the past decade the budget for border enforcement has tripled to $6 million and the number of border agents has doubled to about 12,000.

- According to the Immigration Forum, the cost of making an arrest along the border has increased from $300 in 1992 to $1,700 in 2002, an increase of 467 percent in one decade.

- In 2004 only 30,000 of the 160,000 non-Mexican illegal immigrants caught by the Border Patrol were sent home because the other 130,000 failed to show up for court hearings.

- *Time* magazine reported in 2004 that between October 2003 and August 25, 2004 the U.S. Border Patrol apprehended nearly 1.1 million illegal immigrants.

How America Feels About Immigration

Those born in the United States are more likely to be concerned about illegal immigration than immigrants. Sixty-six percent of nonimmigrants feel government should be more strict on immigration while only 26 percent of immigrants have the same position.

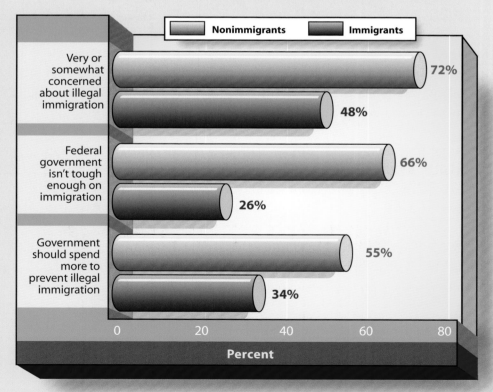

Source: NPR/Kennedy School, *Immigration Survey*, 2004.

Impact of Border Patrol Agents

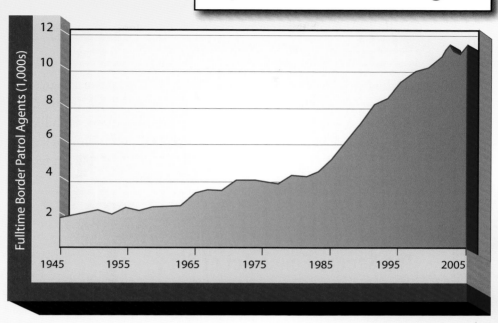

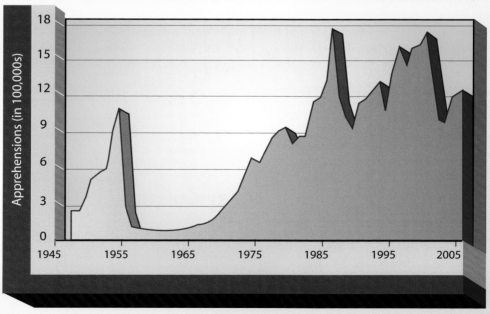

The graphs above show a positive correlation between the number of Border Patrol agents and the number of illegal immigrant apprehensions. Many experts contest that America's borders need more support and that increasing the Border Patrol force will be a major factor in controlling illegal immigration.

Source: Transactional Records Access Clearinghouse, Syracuse University, 2006. http://trac.syr.edu.

- Between 1999 and 2003, work-site immigration enforcement operations were scaled back 95 percent by the federal government. In 2004 ICE issued only three notices of intent to fine employers who were found to be guilty of hiring illegal workers.

- According to a 2005 study by the Center for American Progress, it would cost about $41 billion a year to remove illegal immigrants from America—$28 billion per year to apprehend them, $6 billion a year to detain them, $500 million for extra beds, $4 billion to secure borders, $2 million to legally process them, and $1.6 billion to bus or fly them home.

The Secure Fence Act of 2006

In the fall of 2006 President Bush signed a bill approving the construction of fencing along the U.S.-Mexico border. In addition to the fencing, the bill includes the implementation of other security measures such as cameras, lighting, and sensors. Critics claim that increased fencing will slow down illegal crossings but not prevent them.

Source: CNN.com.

Fines Against Employers of Illegal Immigrants

This chart shows the declining enforcement of laws that prohibit the hiring of illegal immigrants. While through the 1990s millions of dollars in employer fines were collected, no fines were collected from 2000–2003. Immigration experts believe that the key to reducing illegal immigration is by targeting the employers who draw and hire them.

Source: INS Statistical Yearbook, Migration Information Source, November 2005.

- In 2005 ICE won 127 criminal convictions and obtained $15 million in settlements from Wal-Mart and 12 of its subcontractors who were found to be hiring illegal workers.

Americans Want Tougher Penalties Placed on Employers

This chart is based on data from a CNN poll conducted in 2006 and indicates that the majority of Americans believe that employers should be discouraged from hiring illegal immigrants by imposing and enforcing tougher penalties.

Would you favor increasing penalties for employers who hire illegal immigrants?

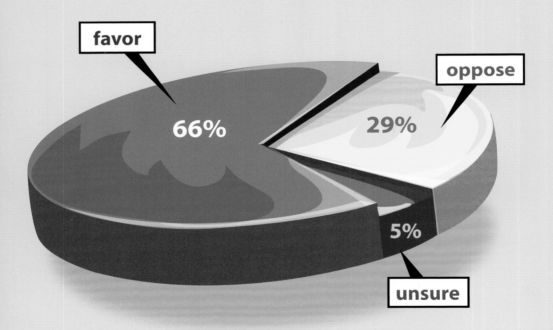

favor 66%

oppose 29%

unsure 5%

Source: CNN poll, May 2006.

How Should America Treat Illegal Immigrants?

> **"The answer to [the illegal immigration] dilemma resides somewhere between the deportation of 12 million illegal immigrants and the declaration that everyone in the world . . . has a God-given right to live here."**
>
> —Thomas L. Bock, "Amnesty Without Assimilation Does Nothing to Help Immigrants," *Hill*, April 26, 2006. www.hillnews.com.

Another important issue in the illegal immigration debate is how America should deal with the approximately 12 million illegal immigrants already in the United States. Many Americans are moved by the poverty, struggle, and hard work of illegal immigrants and believe they should be allowed to stay in the United States but there is also strong support for increasing deportations. An April 2006 CNN poll, for example, found that 77 percent of Americans favor an amnesty program—that is, an award of legal status and a chance to apply for citizenship—for illegal immigrants who have been in the United States for more than five years. According to a June 2006 CNN poll, however, a majority of Americans (67 percent) think illegal immigrants should be deported, or required to return to their home countries. With Congress similarly divided on the issue, millions of illegal immigrants work and live in the United States in a sort of limbo, presenting states and localities with the practical dilemma of how they should be treated in numerous matters ranging from driver's licenses to college tuition rates.

Deportation

By law, because illegal immigrants have entered the United States without visas and in violation of U.S. immigration laws, they are subject to immediate deportation, or forced removal from the United States, at any time. Advocates for illegal immigrants say that this deportable status causes illegal immigrants to live in the shadows, vulnerable to unscrupulous employers and crime. A large number of illegal immigrants have lived in the United States for many years and have established ties to jobs and communities. Millions have borne children here who are now U.S. citizens, while others arrived years ago with small children in tow. Having grown up in this country and attended U.S. schools, many of these children speak only English and know no other life but America. Advocates say it would be inhumane as well as costly to round up and deport these families to their home countries. One study found that mass deportations would cost $206 billion over the next five years.

> Many Americans want the U.S. government to provide amnesty to the illegal immigrants already living in the United States.

Many other Americans, however, resent the fact that foreigners have entered the country in violation of U.S. immigration laws, ahead of those who wait their turn for legal entry. They would like to see all illegal immigrants deported. Fear of deportation is not unfair, these critics argue, because it is the price of entering the country illegally. As policy analyst Heather MacDonald explains: "The bargain they chose was clear: if you come here illegally, the law says that you should face deportation."[42] In fact, some critics suggest that the reason the illegal immigrant population has exploded is precisely because there has been virtually no immigration enforcement and no risk of deportation in recent years.

Amnesty

Instead of stepping up deportations, many Americans want the U.S. government to provide amnesty to the illegal immigrants already living in the United States. Amnesty, also called legalization or normalization, would remove the threat of deportation, provide permanent legal status that would allow illegal immigrants to stay and work permanently in the United States and provide a path to U.S. citizenship. In essence, as the

National Council of La Raza puts it, amnesty would allow illegal immigrants to "come out of the shadows."[43]

The strong push for an amnesty program is supported not only by many Latinos, immigrant rights groups, churches, and others who want to help illegal immigrants, but also by major unions, employers, and many politicians. Unions that represent workers in low-skill industries, such as the Service Employees International Union (SEIU), for example, stand to gain many new members if the current illegal population is given legal status. For employers in these industries, amnesty provides a way to legalize currently illegal workforces. Politicians, meanwhile, can expect campaign contributions from affected businesses and potentially could win millions of Hispanic votes.

This broad support helped to produce the 2006 Senate immigration bill, which proposed a broad amnesty program covering most of the 12 million illegal immigrants now living in the United States. The Senate amnesty proposal had three components. First, illegal immigrants who have lived in the United States for more than five years—approximately 8 million people—could apply for permanent resident status (that is, legal residency as foreign citizens) if they pay back taxes and a $2,000 fine. After five years as legal residents, they can become U.S. citizens as long as they remain employed, learn English, and do not commit crimes. Second, those who have lived here between two and five years—estimated at about 2.8 million—could qualify for a three-year temporary worker status with options for eventually becoming permanent residents and applying for citizenship. Finally, agricultural workers could sign up for a three-year worker status and later apply for permanent status and eventual citizenship. Only illegal immigrants who have been in America less than two years would be subject to immediate deportation. Supporters hailed the Senate bill as a humanitarian success. As Senator Ted Kennedy (D-MA) said, the legislation sent a message to millions of illegal immigrants that "you are going to be welcome, and you won't have to live in fear in the future."[44]

The Effects of Amnesty

No amnesty approach, however, is designed to stem the flow of illegal immigrants into America, and critics of amnesty programs say they might even encourage more illegal immigration. Following the last grant of amnesty in

1986, the numbers of illegal entrants swelled, creating today's large illegal population. As the Coalition for the Future American Worker (CFAW) states, "We granted what was supposed to be a one-time-only amnesty to some 3 million illegal aliens in 1986, only to find that today they have been replaced by an estimated 9–11 million new illegal aliens. Amnesty doesn't cure the problem; it exacerbates it."[45]

Analysts predict that the Senate proposal would produce even more massive increases in illegal immigration than did the 1986 law. Altogether, the Senate proposal would grant amnesty to about 10 million illegal immigrants, more than three times the number of people covered by the 1986 program.

State and Local Benefits

Until the federal government takes some action to resolve the illegal immigrant crisis, however, the reality is that 12 million illegal immigrants will continue to live and work in the United States. Since illegal immigrants, especially those with children, have all the same needs as citizens and legal immigrants—including employment, education, health care, transportation, and housing—this presents state and local officials with the dilemma of how to treat these illegal residents. This situation has resulted in an avalanche of legislative proposals in states and communities around the country. According to the National Conference of State Legislators, 550 immigration-related bills were introduced in 43 states in 2006 alone.

A few state and local governments have adopted policies to help illegal residents. For example, nine states, including California, have decided to offer in-state college tuition rates to the noncitizen children of illegal immigrants. In addition, federal legislation has been proposed to extend college benefits to illegal immigrants on a nationwide basis. The Development, Relief, and Education for Alien Minors (or DREAM) Act was introduced in 2005 (and was included in the 2006 Senate immigration bill), but has not become law. If enacted, DREAM would offer noncitizen children of illegal immigrants permanent resident status, a designation that would allow them to attend U.S. colleges and find jobs after they graduate. As Janet Murguia, president and CEO of the National Council of La Raza, has explained, "The DREAM Act unleashes the enormous potential of thousands of young students, giving them the freedom to dream of a future with genuine educational, job, and life opportunities."[46] Opponents of DREAM argue, however, that it is unfair for illegal immigrant children to be granted legal status and in-state tuition rates, while American citizens from other states are charged full tuition and foreigners who abide by immigration rules must wait for student visas.

State and Local Restrictions

More than thirty state legislatures and local governments, however, have recently placed restrictions on state benefits and rights in order to discourage illegal immigration. Arizona, Colorado, and Georgia, for instance, have all passed sweeping laws that ban illegal residents from receiving state-funded benefits such as health care, energy assistance, adult education, child care, and elderly services. Other states, including Idaho, Missouri, Oklahoma, Kansas, Illinois, and Rhode Island, have passed limited laws to restrict specific state services for illegal residents, such as unemployment or health benefits. California's legislature recently rejected proposals to provide the children of illegal residents with health coverage.

> " A number of cities and states, meanwhile, have acted to prevent illegal immigrants from obtaining jobs and housing. "

A number of cities and states, meanwhile, have acted to prevent illegal immigrants from obtaining jobs and housing. The city of Hazleton, Pennsylvania, made news in July 2006 by passing a law that imposes a $1,000 fine for landlords who provide illegal immigrants with housing and denies business permits to employers who give them jobs. Other cities—such as Farmers Branch, Texas; Riverside, New Jersey; and Escondido, California—have since passed similar ordinances.

Another benefit increasingly restricted at the state level is driver's licenses. In 2003 Californians even mounted a gubernatorial recall election partly over this issue. Then-California governor Gray Davis, who signed legislation granting driver's licenses to illegal immigrant residents, was defeated by Republican challenger Arnold Schwarzenegger, who persuaded the state legislature to repeal the legislation. Other states, such as New York, North Carolina, Maine, and Florida, have recently passed laws requiring that driver's license applicants provide proof of citizenship or legal residency.

Many states, too, frustrated with the federal government's lack of leadership on immigration, have ventured into the area of immigration enforcement. Florida, Alabama, and Massachusetts, for example, have sought federal permission to empower state police to arrest illegal immigrants. A number of other states are targeting employers who hire illegal immigrants. Laws in Colorado, Pennsylvania, and Georgia, for instance, require businesses seeking state contracts to verify the immigration status of workers. Arizona and dozens of cities across the nation have also formally made English the official language.

In addition, a few states, such as New Hampshire and Virginia, have passed laws to require proof of citizenship to vote in state and local elections. Although it is a crime for illegal immigrants to vote in federal or state elections, federal voter registration forms only require voters to attest that they are U.S. citizens, so illegal immigrants may be voting in some American elections. Indeed, in 2006 a California candidate for the U.S. House of Representatives, Kathleen Busby, was recorded urging an undocumented Latino to vote; she advised, "You don't need papers for voting." [47] Like other areas of the illegal immigration debate, the question of how to treat illegal residents in the United States has generated little common ground.

How Should America Treat Illegal Immigrants?

> **Massive deportation of the people here is unrealistic. It's just not going to work.**

—President George W. Bush, speech at the Hyatt Regency Hotel in Irvine, California, "President Discusses Comprehensive Immigration Reform," April 24, 2006.

Bush is the forty-third president of the United States

> **Anything short of [illegal immigrant] deportation is amnesty. And that will be an absolute disaster.**

—Mac Johnson, "Immigration Reform Will Fail Without Deportation," *Human Events Online*, May 8, 2006. www.human eventsonline.com.

Johnson is a writer and medical researcher in Cambridge, Massachusetts, and a regular contributor to *Human Events Online*, a conservative weekly magazine.

> **It's imperative that we join together to provide some type of protections for these 12 million immigrants while we work to establish a guest worker program.**

—John McCain, press release, September 26, 2006. www.mccain.senate.gov.

McCain is a Republican senator from Arizona and an active participant in U.S. immigration policy reform.

* Editor's Note: While the definition of a primary source can be narrowly or broadly defined, for the purposes of Compact Research, a primary source consists of: 1) results of original research presented by an organization or researcher; 2) eyewitness accounts of events, personal experience, or work experience; 3) first-person editorials offering pundits' opinions; 4) government officials presenting political plans and/or policies; 5) representatives of organizations presenting testimony or policy.

❝It is a measure of how surreal our immigration practice has become that it is now 'mean-spirited' simply to raise the possibility in an illegal's mind that his deportation risk is real, much less actually to deport him.❞

—Heather MacDonald, "Illegal Immigration Myths: Cutting Through the Baloney on What to Do About Illegals," *City Journal*, May 1, 2006.

MacDonald is a senior fellow at the Manhattan Institute, a nonprofit public policy group.

❝We reject calls for exploitative "guest worker programs" and call instead for amnesty for all immigrant workers who now reside in the United States.❞

—Joseph G. Ramsey, Dan DiMaggio, and Daniel Brasil Becker, "Support Immigrant Workers' Rights at Tufts and Beyond," May 1, 2006. www.tuftsdaily.com.

Ramsey, DiMaggio, and Becker are students at Tufts University and contributing writers for the *Tufts Daily* newspaper.

❝The 1986 [amnesty] act did not solve our illegal immigration problem. . . . After a six-month slowdown that followed passage of the legislation, illegal immigration . . . continued unabated.❞

—Edwin Meese III, "An Amnesty by Any Other Name . . . ," *New York Times*, May 24, 2006.

Meese III was U.S. attorney-general from 1985 to 1988 during the Ronald Reagan Administration and is currently a fellow at the Heritage Foundation, a conservative think tank.

❝There is absolutely no good reason why any immigrant who comes to this country . . . should be relegated to a repressive, second-class guest worker status.❞

—Linda Chavez Thompson, press release, February 28, 2006, www.aflcio.org.

Chavez Thompson is executive vice-president of the AFL-CIO, a national organization committed to workers' rights and bringing economic justice to the workplace.

❝I was burned once in 1986 when I voted for amnesty believing that it would solve our problems. Now, we have a 12 million illegal immigrant problem.❞

—Charles Grassley, "Grassley Unveils Top 10 Flaws with Amnesty and Guest Worker of Comprehensive Immigration Reform Bill," press release, May 23, 2006. www.grassley.senate.gov.

Grassley is a Republican member of the Senate from Iowa.

❝Deportation or incarceration of the millions who risked death to cross the border illegally . . . is logistically, economically and diplomatically unwise and inhumane.❞

—Thomas L. Bock, "Amnesty Without Assimilation Does Nothing to Help Immigrants," *Hill*, June 23, 2006. www.hillnews.com.

Bock is national commander of the American Legion, the nation's largest military veterans organization.

❝We can secure our borders and continue to welcome immigrants, but we must do so without rewarding illegal behavior with citizenship and voting rights.❞

—Jim Demint, "Amnesty Bill Unfair to Immigrants and Americans," *State*, June 1, 2006. www.thestate.com.

Demint is a Republican member of the U.S. Senate from South Carolina.

66We should not do anything about 'undocumented persons' in the country, it is said, because nations should not make laws closing their borders to anyone in need of a better way of life, and if they do have such laws they are illegitimate and should be ignored as violating international human rights.99

—Otis L. Graham Jr., *Unguarded Gates: A History of America's Immigration Crisis*. New York: Rowman & Littlefield, 2004, p. 182.

Graham Jr. is author and professor emeritus of history at the University of California, Santa Barbara.

66Immigrants . . . want the same thing sought by Black people . . . equal rights, to really belong to the communities where they live, and economic opportunity for their families.99

—David Bacon, "Equality, or Not," Truthout/Perspective, Friday, March 3, 2006. www.truthout.org.

Bacon is a California photojournalist and book author who documents labor, migration, and globalization issues.

How Should America Treat Illegal Immigrants?

- According to a 2006 poll by Zogby International, 52 percent of Americans oppose amnesty for illegal immigrants while 32 percent favor an amnesty program.

- A 2004 study by the Center for Immigration Studies estimated that amnesty for illegal aliens currently living in the United States would create a federal fiscal deficit of nearly $29 billion per year.

- One of the terrorists who participated in the 1993 World Trade Center bombing was given legal status in the 1986 amnesty.

- According to a recent survey of Latinos by the Pew Hispanic Center, six in ten Hispanics born in this country approve of measures to prohibit illegal immigrants from getting driver's licenses.

- The Department of Homeland Security reports that 202,842 illegal immigrants were deported or otherwise expelled from the country in 2004, and 1,053,477 illegal immigrants left voluntarily.

- According to California state congressman Elton Gallegly, California spends nearly $1 billion a year in Medi-Cal services for an average of 780,000 illegal immigrants a month, over and above emergency health services.

Illegal Immigration

Americans Favor Tougher and Enforced Immigration Laws

Based on data from a Zogby poll conducted in 2006 concerning two proposals from Congress on how to treat illegal immigrants, the majority of Americans prefer the tougher House bill that aims to reduce illegal immigration and 12 percent want mass deportations. Hispanic Americans favor the more relaxed U.S. Senate proposal and are 100 percent against mass deportations.

All Americans

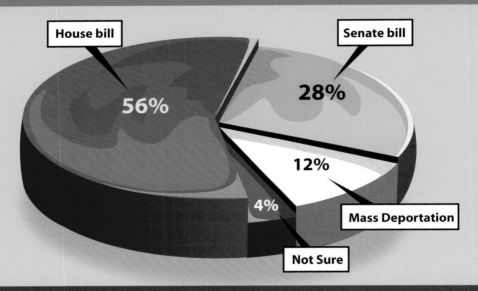

House bill 56%
Senate bill 28%
12% Mass Deportation
4% Not Sure

Hispanics

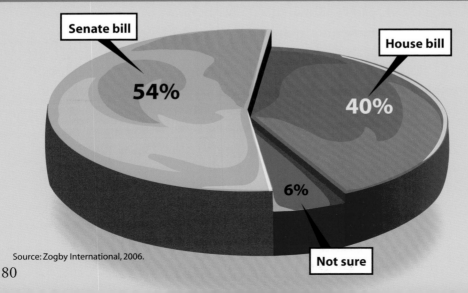

Senate bill 54%
House bill 40%
6% Not sure

- Los Angeles and San Francisco have declared themselves to be sanctuaries where cooperation with federal immigration authorities is disallowed. These sanctuary laws are illegal under the 1996 federal immigration law and a 1999 U.S. Supreme Court ruling, but the federal government does not enforce the matter.

- According to the National Conference of State Legislators, at least 78 bills have been enacted in 33 states in 2006 relating to immigration, a pace that exceeds that of 2005.

American Support for Amnesty of Illegal Immigrants Varies by Age

Based on data from a 2006 Zogby poll, younger Americans are more likely than older Americans to support amnesty for illegal immigrants. Amnesty would remove the threat of deportation, allow illegal immigrants to work in America, and provide a path to U.S. citizenship. Sixty-eight percent of Americans seventy years or older are against amnesty while only 37 percent of 18–24 year olds have the same position.

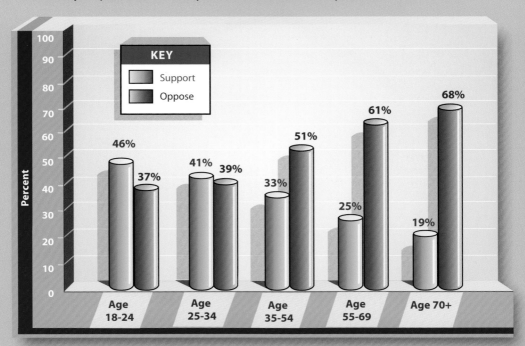

Source: Zogby International, 2006. www.zogby.com.

A Near Majority of Americans Do Not Think It Should Be a Felony to be in the U.S. Illegally

While over half of Americans support tougher immigration laws, they are less certain how to make them tougher. Based on data from a 2006 *Los Angeles Times* and Bloomberg poll regarding immigration reform, only 44 percent of Americans support making illegal immigration a felony while 21 percent were unfamiliar with the proposal.

Do you support or oppose making illegal immigration a felony?

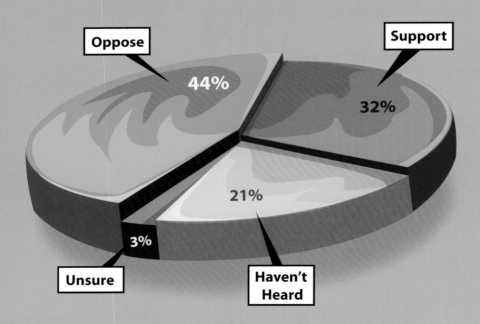

Oppose
44%

Support
32%

21%

3%

Unsure

Haven't Heard

Source: *Los Angeles Times,*/Bloomberg Poll, 2006.

Key People and Advocacy Groups

Roy Beck: Author and former journalist Beck is currently the executive director of Numbers USA, a nonprofit, nonpartisan, public policy organization that opposes high levels of immigration. Beck devotes himself to writing, speaking, and testifying before Congress about immigration issues.

George Borjas: A professor of economics and social policy at the John F. Kennedy School of Government, Harvard University, Borjas is considered one of the nation's leading experts on immigration. Cuban-born, Borjas immigrated to the United States in 1962. He is the author of the 1999 book *Heaven's Door: Immigration Policy and the American Economy*, which argues for reducing U.S. immigration levels.

Pat Buchanan: An American author, syndicated columnist, and television commentator, Buchanan is known as a political conservative. In his writings and commentary, he has taken very strong positions warning of the need to stop illegal immigration. He is the author of a 2006 book on the subject of illegal immigration, *State of Emergency: The Third World Invasion and Conquest of America.*

George W. Bush: A Republican elected forty-third president of the United States in 2000 and 2004, Bush in a nationwide speech in May 2005, called for a comprehensive approach to illegal immigration that combined tougher border and work-site enforcement with a guest worker program. Bush also proposed sending National Guard troops to the U.S.-Mexico border.

David Card: A professor of economics at the University of California, Berkeley, Card specializes in labor economics and has researched and written a number of scholarly papers on immigration issues, including a January 2005 paper titled "Is Immigration So Bad?"

Lou Dobbs: A Harvard-educated economist and editorial columnist, Dobbs is also the anchor of CNN's nightly television show, *Lou Dobbs Tonight*. He has become well known for his in-depth reporting and analysis on the issue of illegal immigration.

Vicente Fox: Fox was elected president of Mexico in 2000. During his term, which ended in 2006, he spoke out in favor of a comprehensive U.S. immigration policy that would include an amnesty program to award U.S. citizenship to illegal immigrants living in the United States.

Bill Frist: A Republican senator from Tennessee, Bill Frist was elected to the Senate in 1994 after a career as a heart and lung transplant surgeon. He was reelected in 2000 and in 2003 became the Senate majority leader, a role that placed him in the center of the Senate's immigration reform debate in 2006.

Jim Gilchrist: A former Marine, newspaper reporter, and certified public accountant, Gilchrist is the founder of the Minuteman Project, a group of citizens that want to halt illegal immigration and force the federal government to enforce U.S. immigration laws. Gilchrist writes and speaks frequently on the subject of illegal immigration.

Daniel T. Griswold: Griswold is associate director of the Center for Trade Policy Studies, a project of the Cato Institute, a libertarian policy organization that supports limited government, individual liberty, and free markets. Griswold frequently writes and speaks on immigration topics and is a supporter of liberal immigration policies.

J. Dennis Hastert: A Republican from Illinois, Hastert has been a member of the U.S. House of Representatives since 1986 and was Speaker of the House from 1999 to 2006. In this position, he played a key role in the Congressional efforts to enact immigration reform.

Antonia Hernandez: As president and general counsel of MALDEF, a leading Latino and immigrant rights organization, Hernandez has been a life-long advocate for Latino civil rights. She speaks frequently on issues relating to illegal immigrants.

Bill Ong Hing: A professor of law and Asian American studies at the University of California, Davis, Bill Ong Hing is also a leading expert on immigration issues. His books include *Defining America Through Immigration Policy* (2004), *To Be an American: Cultural Pluralism and the Rhetoric of Assimilation* (1997), and *Making and Remaking Asian America Through Immigration Policy* (1990).

John Hostettler: A Republican from Indiana, Hostettler has been chair of the House Subcommittee on Immigration, Border Security, and Claims since 2003. In this position, he helped to pass the 2005 House bill on immigration reform.

Samuel P. Huntington: A distinguished professor of political science at Harvard, Huntington wrote "The Clash of Civilizations," a controversial 1993 essay that predicted that people's cultural and religious conflicts, not ideological or economic differences would be the primary challenge in foreign affairs in the future. In 2004 Huntington wrote *Who Are We? The Challenges to America's National Identity*, a book that argues that Hispanic immigration is undermining U.S. culture. He has also written numerous articles on immigration.

Edward "Ted" M. Kennedy: A prominent Democrat and U.S. senator from Massachusetts since 1962, Kennedy is a longtime supporter of liberal immigration policies. In 2006 he cosponsored an immigration reform bill with Senator John McCain (R-AZ) that formed the basis for the bipartisan Comprehensive Immigration Reform Act, a bill that passed the Senate in May 2006.

Mark Krikorian: As executive director of the Center for Immigration Studies, a think tank devoted to research and policy analysis of the economic, social, demographic, fiscal, and other impacts of immigration on the United States, Krikorian is a leading advocate of reducing immigration levels in the United States. He often testifies before Congress, and he has written numerous articles on illegal immigration.

Michelle Malkin: A journalist and syndicated columnist, Malkin launched a political blog, michellemalkin.com, in 2004, and is an outspoken critic of the federal government's immigration enforcement efforts. She also has written the book *Invasion: How America Still Welcomes Terrorists, Criminals, and Other Foreign Menaces to Our Shores*.

Cecilia Muñoz: Muñoz is vice president of research, advocacy, and legislation of the National Council of La Raza (NCLR), a Hispanic civil rights and advocacy group. As NCLR's chief lobbyist, she has been a prominent voice on the topic of illegal immigration, often testifying before Congress and commenting on news programs about the subject.

Jeffrey Passel: Passel is a principal research associate at the Urban Institute, an independent, nonpartisan research and advisory organization devoted to the study of problems facing American cities. Passel's research has focused on the impact of immigrants on and their integration into American society and the demography of immigration, particularly the measurement of illegal immigration.

Harry Reid: A Democratic senator from Nevada since 1986, Reid began his congressional career when he was elected to the House of Representatives in 1982. He became the Senate minority leader in 2005 and helped pass a Senate immigration reform bill in 2006.

James Sensenbrenner: A Republican member of the U.S. House of Representatives, Sensenbrenner will be the top-ranking House negotiator assigned to resolve any differences between House and Senate bills affecting immigration.

Robert Suro: Formerly an overseas correspondent for the *New York Times*, Suro is currently director of the Pew Hispanic Center, a nonpartisan research organization that tracks the impact of Latinos in the United States. He also is the author of *Strangers Among Us*, a book about how the Latino population is changing America.

Thomas G. Tancredo: A Republican member of the House of Representatives from Colorado, Tancredo has supported a reduction of immigration for many years. In 2006 Tancredo spoke out repeatedly against illegal immigration and has suggested that he may run for president in 2008 on an anti-immigration platform.

Linda Chavez Thompson: Chavez Thompson has held various positions in Republican administrations and today is a prominent Hispanic-American conservative author, radio talk show host, and Fox News commentator. She frequently writes and speaks about illegal immigration.

Chronology

1830–1930
Twenty seven million immigrants travel to the United States from Germany, Ireland, Russia, Italy, and various parts of central and eastern Europe, China, and Japan.

1892–1954
Ellis Island, in New York Bay, served as the chief immigration station in the United States. It is estimated that 40 percent of all Americans had an ancestor arrive at Ellis Island.

1965
The Hart-Celler Immigration Act is enacted, sharply cutting back Western and Northern European immigrants and resulting in large increases in Hispanic and Asian immigration.

1830	1920	1930	1940	1950	1960	1970	1980

1924
The Johnson-Reed Act, the nation's first comprehensive immigration bill, is enacted to restrict the numbers of immigrants.

1964
The Bracero Program ends, but Mexican workers continue to enter the United States illegally to work in agriculture.

1986
The Immigration Reform and Control Act (IRCA) is enacted. It raises the annual immigration ceiling, creates employer sanctions to punish employers for "knowingly" hiring illegal workers, and provides amnesty to almost 3 million illegal immigrants.

1942
The Bracero Program encourages 4.8 million Mexican laborers to enter the United States temporarily to work in agriculture to help ease manpower shortages during World War II.

1986–1996

The number of illegal immigrants rises steeply following the 1986 amnesty program.

2003

The U.S. Immigration and Naturalization Service (INS) becomes part of the Department of Homeland Security (DHS) with immigration enforcement moving to the new U.S. Immigration and Customs Enforcement (ICE).

2005

The U.S. House of Representatives passes its version of a bill that focuses on enforcement, and provides for seven hundred miles of border fencing and for a new system of employer sanctions with electronic verification of employee identification documents.

1990   1995   2000   2005

2004

The number of illegal immigrants living in the United States grows to between 7 and 20 million.

1996

Congress votes to double the U.S. Border Patrol to ten thousand agents over five years and mandates the construction of fences at the most heavily trafficked areas of the U.S.-Mexico border. President Bill Clinton signs a welfare reform bill that cuts many social programs for illegal immigrants.

2006

Congress enacts the Secure Fence Act, which provides seven hundred miles of fencing along the U.S.-Mexico border.

May 1: Several million people, most of them of Latino heritage and many of them believed to be illegal immigrants, staged marches and protests in cities across the United States in support of illegal immigrant workers' rights.

Related Organizations

American Immigration Law Foundation (AILF)

918 F St. NW, 6th Floor

Washington, DC 20004

phone: (202) 742-5600

fax: (202) 742-5619

e-mail: info@ailf.org

Web site: www.ailf.org.

The AILF is a tax-exempt, nonprofit educational and charitable organization dedicated to increasing public understanding of immigration law and policy and the value of immigration to American society. One of its programs is the Immigration Policy Center (IPC), a think tank that does research and analysis on immigration topics. The IPC publishes the monthly *Immigration Policy In Focus* as well as numerous other publications on immigration topics.

Center for Immigration Studies (CIS)

1522 K St. NW, Suite 820

Washington, DC 20005-1202

phone: (202) 466-8185

fax: (202) 466-8076

e-mail: center@cis.org

Web site: www.cis.org

The Center for Immigration Studies is an independent, nonpartisan think tank that advocates for reduced immigration and is devoted to research and policy analysis of the economic, social, demographic, fiscal, and other impacts of immigration on the United States. CIS publishes background papers and other reports, such as "Attrition Through Enforcement: A Cost-Effective Strategy to Shrink the Illegal Population" and "An Examination of U.S. Immigration Policy and Serious Crime."

Essential Worker Immigration Coalition (EWIC)

1615 H St. NW

Washington, DC 20062

phone: (202) 463-5931

Web site: ewic@uschamber.com

EWIC includes businesses, trade associations, and other organizations that advocate immigration policies that facilitate the employment of essential workers by U.S. companies. It has two main goals: to reform the immigration system to allow employers to bring in foreign workers when no American workers can be found and to create a mechanism for many of the millions of undocumented workers in the United States to earn legal status.

Federation for American Immigration Reform (FAIR)

1666 Connecticut Ave. NW, Suite 400

Washington, DC 20009

phone: (202) 328-7004

fax: (202) 387-3447

Web site: www.fairus.org

FAIR is a national nonprofit public-interest membership organization of concerned citizens dedicated to reforming the nation's immigration policies. FAIR seeks to improve border security, to stop illegal immigration, and to reduce immigration levels to about three hundred thousand a year. Its comprehensive Web site includes reports such as "Immigration and Income Inequality: How Rising Immigration Leads to the Declining Share of Middle-Income Households and Greater Income Inequality" and "The Sinking Lifeboat: Uncontrolled Immigration and the U.S. Health Care System."

Heritage Foundation

214 Massachusetts Ave. NE

Washington DC 20002-4999

phone: (202) 546-4400

fax: (202) 546-8328

Web site: www.heritage.org

The Heritage Foundation is a conservative research and educational think tank devoted to formulating and promoting public policies based on the principles of free enterprise, limited government, individual freedom, traditional American values, and a strong national defense. The group's Web site contains numerous articles on the subject of immigration.

The Latino Coalition (TLC)

707 Fifth St. SE

Washington, DC 20003

phone: (202) 546-0008

fax: (202) 546-0807

e-mail: info@thelatinocoalition.org

Web site: www.thelatinocoalition.com

The Latino Coalition is a membership organization that promotes policies relevant to Latinos' overall economic, cultural, and social development. TLC monitors public policy at the federal, state, and local levels and conducts public education programs to raise awareness of the impact of these policies on Latino communities in the United States.

Mexican American Legal Defense and Education Fund (MALDEF)

1717 K St. NW, #311

Washington, DC 20036

phone: (202) 293-2828

fax: (202) 293-2849

Web site: www.maldef.org

MALDEF is a nonprofit Latino litigation, advocacy, and educational outreach institution dedicated to fostering public policies, laws, and programs to safeguard the civil rights of Latinos living in the United States. Its Web site contains a section on immigration that outlines the efforts and successes of the group's Immigrants' Rights Program and lists various publications on the immigration issue.

The Minuteman Project

Attn: Jim Gilchrist

PO Box 3944

Laguna Hills, CA 92654-3944

phone: (949) 222-4266

fax: (949) 222-6607

Web site: www.minutemanproject.com

The Minuteman Project is a citizen vigilance committee set up to monitor immigration, business, and government. It opposes illegal immigration through nonviolent citizen patrols in support of effective U.S. immigration law enforcement. Its Web site contains press releases and other information about the group's activities and the illegal immigration issue.

National Council of La Raza (NCLR)

1126 Sixteenth St. NW, Raul Yzaguirre Bldg.

Washington, DC 20036

phone: (202) 785-1670

fax: (202) 776-1792

e-mail: comments@nclr.org

Web site: www.nclr.org

The NCLR is a civil rights and advocacy organization that works to improve opportunities for Hispanic Americans. NCLR conducts research, policy analysis, and advocacy on behalf of Latinos in five key areas: assets/investments, education, employment and economic status, health, and civil rights/immigration. Its Web site provides updates on immigration reform efforts and other information relevant to the illegal immigration issue.

National Immigration Forum

50 F St. NW, Suite 300

Washington, DC 20001

phone: (202) 347-0040

fax: (202) 347-0058

Web site: www.immigrationforum.org

The National Immigration Forum is an immigrant rights organization that is dedicated to embracing and upholding America's tradition as a nation of immigrants. It advocates for public policies that welcome immigrants and refugees and support the reunification of families, the rescue and resettlement of refugees fleeing persecution, and the equal treatment of immigrants under the law. Its Web site offers publications such as "Immigration Basics" and "Basic Immigration Facts," and provides analysis of the immigration issue.

National Network for Immigrant and Refugee Rights (NNIRR)

310 Eighth St., Suite 303

Oakland, CA 94607

phone: (510) 465-1984

fax: (510) 465-1885

e-mail: nnirr@nnirr.org

Web site: www.nnirr.org

NNIRR is a national organization composed of local coalitions and immigrant, refugee, community, religious, civil rights, and labor organizations and activists. It advocates a just U.S. immigration policy and seeks to protect the rights of immigrants, regardless of immigration status.

NumbersUSA

1601 N. Kent St., Suite 1100

Arlington, VA 22209

phone: (703) 816-8820

Web site: www.numbersusa.com

NumbersUSA is a nonprofit, nonpartisan, public policy organization that opposes high levels of immigration and seeks to educate the public about immigration numbers and the recommendations about immigration from two national commissions of the 1990s. The group's Web site offers studies and reports as free downloads, including *The Case Against Immigration,* by executive director Roy Beck.

Pew Hispanic Center

1615 L St. NW, Suite 700

Washington, DC 20036-5610

phone: (202) 419-3600

fax: (202) 419-3608

e-mail: info@pewhispanic.org

Web site: http://pewhispanic.org

The Pew Hispanic Center is a nonpartisan research organization that seeks to improve understanding of the U.S. Hispanic population and to chronicle Latinos' growing impact on the nation. The center is a project of the Pew Research Center, a nonpartisan "fact tank" that provides information on the issues, attitudes, and trends shaping America and the world. It publishes numerous reports and research studies on the immigration issue; recent publications include "Modes of Entry for the Unauthorized Migrant Population" and "America's Immigration Quandary: No Consensus on Immigration Problem or Proposed Fixes."

Public Policy Institute of California (PPIC)

500 Washington St., Suite 800

San Francisco, California 94111

phone: (415) 291-4400

fax: (415) 291-4401

Web site: www.ppic.org

The PPIC is a research organization dedicated to improving public policy in California. Its research program focuses on three areas: population, economy, and governance and public finance. The PPIC Web site contains publications such as "Just the Facts: Immigrants in California" and "Holding the Line? The Effect of Recent Border Build-Up on Unauthorized Immigration."

Service Employees International Union (SEIU)

1313 L St. NW

Washington, DC 20005

phone: (202) 898-3200

Web site: www.seiu.org

The SEIU is a national labor union that represents workers in hospitals, long-term care facilities, property services, and public services. It has been a leading voice for immigration reform that improves conditions for immigrant workers. SEIU's positions on immigration reform and publications such as "Immigrant Workers: Making Valuable Contributions to Our Communities and Our Economy" can be found on its Web site.

U.S. Citizenship and Immigration Services (USCIS)

20 Massachusetts Ave. NW

Washington, DC 20529

(800) 375-5283

Web site: www.uscis.gov

The USCIS is a bureau of the Department of Homeland Security (DHS) and performs many of the administrative functions formerly carried out by the U.S. Immigration and Naturalization Service (INS), which was abolished on March 1, 2003, by the Homeland Security Act of 2002. USCIS is charged with responsibilities such as processing immigrant visa petitions and providing other immigration services; its Web site contains links to DHS immigration enforcement entities, including U.S. Immigration and Customs Enforcement (ICE) and U.S. Customs and Border Protection (CBP).

U.S. Conference of Catholic Bishops (USCCB)

3211 Fourth St. NE

Washington, DC 20017

phone: (800) 235-8722

fax: (202) 722-8709

Web site: www.usccb.org

The USCCB is an assembly of Catholic bishops who work to unify, coordinate, promote, and carry on Catholic Church activities in the United States. The USCCB supports amnesty to provide a path to citizenship for illegal immigrants living in the United States.

For Further Research

Books

Peter Andreas, *Border Games: Policing the U.S.-Mexico Divide*. Ithaca, NY: Cornell University Press, 2000.

George J. Borjas, *Heaven's Door: Immigration Policy and the American Economy*. Princeton, NJ: Princeton University Press, 1999.

Patrick J. Buchanan, *State of Emergency: The Third World Invasion and Conquest of America*. New York: St. Martin's, 2006.

Jim Gilchrist and Jerome Corsi, *Minutemen: The Battle to Secure America's Borders*. Torrance, CA: World Ahead, 2006.

Helen Hayes, *U.S. Immigration Policy and the Undocumented: Ambivalent Laws, Furtive Lives*. Westport, CT: Praeger, 2001.

J.D. Hayworth, *Whatever It Takes: Illegal Immigration, Border Security, and the War on Terror*. Washington, DC: Regnery, 2006.

Bill Ong Hing, *Defining America Through Immigration Policy*. Philadelphia: Temple University Press, 2004.

Samuel P. Huntington, *Who Are We? The Challenges to America's National Identity*. New York: Simon & Schuster, 2004.

Peter Laufer, *Wetback Nation: The Case for Opening the Mexican-American Border*, Chicago: Ivan R. Dee, 2004.

Joseph Nevins, *Operation Gatekeeper: The Rise of the "Illegal Alien" and the Remaking of the U.S.-Mexico Boundary*. New York: Routledge, 2002.

Mae M. Ngai, *Impossible Subjects: Illegal Immigration and the Making of Modern America*. Princeton, NJ: Princeton University Press, 2004.

Tom Tancredo, *In Mortal Danger: The Battle for America's Border and Security*. Nashville, TN: WND, 2006.

Periodicals

Donald L. Barlett and James B. Steele, "Who Left the Door Open?" *Time*, September 20, 2004.

Gary Becker, "The Wise Way to Stem Illegal Immigration," *Business Week*, April 26, 2004.

Ross Douthat and Jenny Woodson, "The Border: Illegal Immigration Is Once Again a Potent Political Issue," *Atlantic Monthly*, January/February 2006.

Maria Echaveste, "Target Employers: For Comprehensive Immigration Reform to Work, Employers Need to Feel the Heat," *American Prospect*, November 2005.

James Goldsborough, "Out-of-Control Immigration," *Foreign Affairs*, September/October 2000.

Tamar Jacoby, "Borderline—Why We Can't Stop Illegal Immigration," *New Republic*, January 26, 2004.

Peter Laufer, "My New Kentucky Home: The Cutting Edge of Illegal Immigration Used to Be Los Angeles. Now It's Owensboro," *Washington Monthly*, January/February 2005.

John Leo, "Citizenship on the Cheap," *U.S. News & World Report*, September 22, 2003.

Jim Lo Scalzo, "A Line in the Sand," *U.S. News & World Report*, March 20, 2006.

Roger Lowenstein, "The Immigration Equation," *New York Times Magazine*, July 9, 2006.

Enrico Marcelli, "Immigrants and the U.S. Labor Market," *NACLA Report on the Americas*, March/April 2005.

Doris Meissner, "Learning from History: As Congress Seeks a Comprehensive Immigration Fix, the Lessons of 1986's Historic Reform Must Guide the Way," *American Prospect*, November 2005.

Jennifer Roback Morse, "When Jobs Are Illegal, Only Illegals Will Have Jobs," *Reason*, May 2004.

Janet Murguia and Cecilia Muñoz, "From Immigrant to Citizen: Most Still Want to Become Americans. Unlike in Past Eras, Though, Our Government Is Doing Far Too Little to Integrate Them into U.S. Society," *American Prospect*, November 2005.

National Catholic Reporter, "Churches Take Immigration Reform Fight into the Streets," March 31, 2006.

————, "The Immigration Dilemma," January 13, 2006.

Ramesh Ponnuru, "Illegal Detour: Thinking Reasonably About Immigration," *National Review*, March 27, 2006.

Marta Tienda, "Be Our Guest? Our Economy Benefits from Immigrants. But If Guest Workers Are Treated as a Caste Without Rights, Native Workers and Immigrants Will Both Suffer," *American Prospect*, November 2005.

Andre Traversa, "Why Conservatives Should Oppose the Anti-Immigration Movement," *World & I*, September 2004.

A.R. Williams, "Latinos Rise Nationwide: America's New Majority Minority," *National Geographic*, November 2003.

Internet Sources

Close-Up Foundation, "U.S. Immigration Policy," 2005. www.closeup.org/immigrat.htm.

Samuel P. Huntington, "The Special Case of Mexican Immigration," *American Enterprise Online*, December 2000. www.taemag.com/issues/articleid.12114/article.detail.asp.

Pew Hispanic Center, "America's Immigration Quandary: No Consensus on Immigration Problem or Proposed Fixes," March 30, 2006. http://pewhispanic.org/reports/report.php?ReportID=63.

Time, "America's Border," September 20, 2004. www.time.com/time/covers/1101040920.

U.S. Commission on Immigration Reform, "Report to Congress: Becoming an American; Immigration and Immigrant Policy," September 1997. www.utexas.edu/lbj/uscir/reports.html.

Washington Post, "The Battle over Immigration," March 31, 2006. www.washingtonpost.com/wp-dyn/content/custom/2006/03/31/CU2006033101407.html.

Source Notes

Overview: Illegal Immigrants in America

1. Quoted in Louis Freedberg and Ramon G. McLeod, "The Other Side of the Law: Despite All U.S. Efforts to Curb It, Immigration Is Rising," *San Francisco Chronicle*, October 13, 1998. www.sfgate.com.
2. Quoted in Otis L. Graham Jr., *Unguarded Gates: A History of America's Immigration Crisis*. Lanham, MD: Rowman & Littlefield, 2004, p. 109.
3. Quoted in Graham, *Unguarded Gates*, p. 108.
4. Quoted in Randy Hall, "Enforcement Key to True Immigration Reform, Panel Says," *Nation*, April 24, 2006. www.cnsnews.com.
5. Samuel P. Huntington, "The Special Case of Mexican Immigration," *American Enterprise Online*, December 2000. www.taemag.com.
6. Quoted in Alexandra Marks, "A Harder Look at Visa Overstayers," *Christian Science Monitor*, February 5, 2002. www.csmonitor.com.
7. Art Moore, "Is Mexico Reconquering U.S. Southwest?" *WorldNetDaily.com*, January 4, 2002. www.worldnetdaily.com.
8. Geri Smith, "Channeling the Remittance Flood," *BusinessWeek Online*, December 28, 2005. www.businessweek.com.
9. John Mendez, "Illegal Immigration: Mexico's Shame," *American Thinker*, May 5, 2006. www.americanthinker.com.

Does Illegal Immigration Harm the U.S. Economy?

10. Carolyn Said, "The Immigration Debate: Effect on Economy Depends on Viewpoint," *San Francisco Chronicle*, May 21 2006. www.sfgate.com.
11. Said, "The Immigration Debate.
12. *BusinessWeek Online*, "Embracing Illegals," July 18, 2005. www.businessweek.com.
13. Quoted in Chris Isidore, "Illegal Workers: Good for U.S. Economy," *CNNMoney.com*, May 1, 2006. http://money.cnn.com.
14. Quoted in Laura Parker, "USA Just Wouldn't Work Without Immigrant Labor," *USA Today*, July 23, 2001. www.usatoday.com.
15. George J. Borjas, "Increasing the Supply of Labor Through Immigration: Measuring the Impact on Native-Born Workers," Center for Immigration Studies, May 2004. www.cis.org.
16. David Card, "Is the New Immigration Really So Bad?" Department of Economics, University of California, Berkeley, January 2005. www.phil.frb.org.
17. Quoted in Parker, "USA Just Wouldn't Work Without Immigrant Labor."
18. Michael S. Dukakis and Daniel J.B. Mitchell, "Raise Wages, Not Walls," *New York Times*, July 25, 2006.
19. Quoted in Michelle Goldberg, "The Left Splits over Immigration," *Salon*, April 20, 2006. www.salon.com.
20. Shikha Dalmia, "Illegal Immigrants Are Paying a Lot More Taxes than You Think," Knight Ridder/Tribune News Service, May 1, 2006. www.reason.org.
21. Quoted in *CouplesCompany.com*, "Cost of Educating Illegal Alien Children in US? $7.4 Billion per Year," August 20, 2003. www.couplescompany.com.
22. Fox News, "L.A. Emergency Rooms Full of Illegal Immigrants," March 18, 2005. www.foxnews.com.

Does Illegal Immigration Threaten American Society?

23. Emma Lazarus, "The New Colossus," reprinted at American Park Network, History: Statue of Liberty, 2001. www.americanparknetwork.com.

24. Quoted in Alvaro Vargas Llosa, "Immigration—the Wages of Fear," Independent Institute, May 19, 2006. www.independent.org.

25. A.R. Williams, "Latinos Rise Nationwide: America's New Majority Minority," *National Geographic,* vol. 204, no. 5, November 2003, p. 4.

26. SUSPS, "U.S. Population and the Environment," 2006. www.susps.org.

27. Quoted in Greg Simmons, "Immigration's Effect on Economy Is Murky," Fox News, March 30, 2006. www.foxnews.com.

28. Heather MacDonald, "Immigration and the Alien Gang Epidemic: Problems and Solutions," testimony before the House Judiciary Subcommittee on Immigration, Border Security, and Claims, April 13, 2005. www.manhattan-institute.org.

29. Quoted in John Perazzo, "Illegal Immigration and Terrorism," *FrontPageMagazine.com,* December 18, 2002. www.frontpagemag.com.

How Should the Government Respond to Illegal Immigration?

30. David S. Broder, "Bush's Tough Sale on Immigration," *San Diego Union-Tribune,* May 18, 2006.

31. Quoted in Tyche Hendricks, "Border Security or Boondoggle? A Plan for 700 Miles of Mexican Border Wall Heads for Senate—Its Future Is Not Assured," *San Francisco Chronicle,* February 26, 2006. www.sfgate.com.

32. Quoted in Will Weissart, "National Guard Can't Close Mexico-US border, Migrants and Experts Say," Associated Press, May 17, 2006. http://legalsoapbox.freeadvice.com.

33. Mark Krikorian, "Visa Overstays: Can We Bar the Terrorist Door?" statement before the U.S. House of Representatives Committee on International Relations, Subcommittee on Oversight and Investigations, May 11, 2006. www.house.gov.

34. Quoted in Hendricks, "Border Security or Boondoggle?"

35. James R. Edwards Jr., "Two Sides of the Same Coin: The Connection Between Legal and Illegal Immigration," Center for Immigration Studies, February 2006. www.cis.org.

36. David Bacon, "No Immigration Bill Is Better," *Truthout,* May 26, 2006. www.afsc.org.

37. Sasha Khokha, "Paper Chase: Immigrant Rights and Undocumented Workers," *NFG Reports,* vol. 8, no. 3, Fall 2001, ww.nfg.org.

38. Quoted in Khokha, "Paper Chase."

39. American Civil Liberties Union, "ACLU Opposes National ID System and Computer Registry," press release, September 11, 1995. www.theforbiddenknowledge.com.

40. Quoted in Esther Pan, "The U.S. Immigration Debate," Council on Foreign Relations, March 22, 2006. www.cfr.org.

41. Philip Martin and Michael Teitelbaum, "The Mirage of Mexican Guest Workers," *Foreign Affairs,* November/December 2001, p. 117.

How Should America Treat Illegal Immigrants?

42. Heather MacDonald, "Illegal Immigration Myths: Cutting Through the Baloney on What to Do About Illegals," *City Journal*, May 1, 2006. www.city-journal.org.

43. National Council of La Raza, "Immigration Reform," 2006. www.nclr.org.

44. Quoted in Jonathan Weisman, "Senate Pact Offers Permits to Most Illegal Immigrants," *Washington Post,* April 7, 2006. www.washingtonpost.com.

45. Coalition for the Future American Worker, "An Amnesty by Any Other Name Is Still an Amnesty," 2006.

www.americanworker.org.

46. Quoted in Pepe Lozano, "DREAM Act Renews Hope for Immigrant Students," *People's Weekly World,* February 2, 2006. www.pww.org.

47. Quoted in Jim Kouri, "Democrat Caught Advising Illegal Aliens to Vote," *Conservative Voice,* June 5, 2006. www.theconservativevoice.com.

List of Illustrations

List of Illustrations

Index

About the Author

Debra A. Miller is a writer and lawyer with a passion for current events and history. She began her law career in Washington, D.C., where she worked on legislative, policy, and legal matters in government, public interest, and private law firm positions. She now lives with her husband in Encinitas, California. She has written and edited numerous books and anthologies on historical and political topics.

DATE DUE

FOLLETT